THE EUROPEAN UNION AND THE COMMONWEALTH CARIBBEAN

The European Union and the Commonwealth Caribbean

Edited by

STEPHEN J.H. DEARDEN
Manchester Metropolitan University

Ashgate

Published by
Ashgate Publishing Limited
Gower House
Croft Road
Aldershot
Hampshire GU11 3HR
England

Ashgate Publishing Company
131 Main Street
Burlington, VT 05401-5600 USA

Ashgate website: http://www.ashgate.com

British Library Cataloguing in Publication Data
The European Union and the Commonwealth Caribbean
1.European Union countries - Commerce - Caribbean Area
2.Caribbean Area - Commerce - European Union countries
I.Dearden, Stephen J. H.
337.4'0729

Library of Congress Control Number: 2001097261

ISBN 0 7546 1794 7

Printed and bound by Athenaeum Press, Ltd.,
Gateshead, Tyne & Wear.

Contents

List of Contributors

Peter Clegg, University of West of England

Stephen Dearden, Manchester Metropolitan University

Anna Dickson, Durham University

Tidings Ndhlovu, Manchester Metropolitan University

Introduction

STEPHEN DEARDEN

This book brings together the work of a number of members of the European Development Policy Study Group of the Development Studies Association. It focuses upon the Commodity Protocols of the European Union that are of particular significance for the Commonwealth Caribbean States. As members of the African Caribbean and Pacific (ACP) group of States, they benefit from both trade concessions and development assistance from the European Union, first under the Lomé Conventions and then under the Cotonou Agreement.

Three Commodity Protocols are of particular significance to these economies - Banana, Sugar and Rum - but each differs in a number of important respects. Rum, for example, has no specific list of ACP beneficiaries, while the Sugar Agreement is a separate Treaty, unrelated to the Lomé Conventions and with no finite life. But all the Commodity Protocols have their origins in the need to accommodate United Kingdom Commonwealth Preferences on the accession of the country to the EC in 1973, and all have a future that is being determined by the demands of the World Trade Organisation (WTO).

In some ways this book is an epitaph to these Agreements. The Rum Protocol has effectively been terminated by a bi-lateral agreement between the EU and the United States as part of the Uruguay Round negotiations of the GATT/WTO, while the Banana Protocol has become the centrepiece of a major trade dispute between the US and EU which challenged the whole future of the Lomé Conventions. In response the successor Cotonou Agreement lays the groundwork for a major change in the trade concessions offered to the middle-income ACP States, which includes the Commonwealth Caribbean, requiring a transition to a reciprocal WTO-compatible trade relationship.

This book begins with a review of the trade and aid dimensions of the Lomé Conventions and assesses their overall impact upon the development of the ACP States. The weaknesses of the Conventions are identified and the successor Cotonou Agreement outlined and appraised. The book then turns specifically to the States of the Commonwealth Caribbean, reviewing their economic performance and the focus of EC aid.

Three groups are examined - the Continental States (Belize, and Guyana); the larger island economies (the Bahamas, Jamaica, Trinidad and Tobago) and the smaller islands (Antigua & Barbuda, Grenada, St. Kitts & Nevis, St. Lucia, St. Vincent and the Grenadines and the British Dependencies).

Chapters Three and Four consider the Banana Protocol. As already suggested, this Protocol is important beyond its significance for a particular industry or State, although for a number of Caribbean islands banana production remains the bedrock of their economies. The dispute with the United States government, acting on behalf of their large multi-national companies that dominate much of the world banana market, has resulted in major changes to the EU's Banana Regime as well as influencing the Cotonou Agreement. Chapter Three describes the nature of the EU banana market and outlines its importance for some of the Caribbean States. It traces the evolution of the EU's Banana Regime, including the latest developments in this ongoing saga, and evaluates the impact of these changes upon the economic development of a number of the island economies. Chapter Four offers a political case study of the negotiations that led to the initial adoption of the EU's Banana Protocol with the creation of the Single Market and its subsequent challenge before the WTO. It highlights the success of the lobbying strategy adopted by the Commonwealth Caribbean within the context of the EU's process of policy formation, but their subsequent marginalisation as the focus of negotiations moved into the orbit of the WTO.

Chapter Five turns to the Sugar Protocol and reviews the reasons for the emergence of international intervention in the world sugar market in general and the Commonwealth Sugar Agreement in particular. It considers the difficulties that presented themselves when this Agreement had to be reconciled with the EC's sugar policy under the CAP at the UK's accession to the Community. The conflict between the interests of the EC's sugar beet producers and the ACP sugar cane exporters continued to be at the heart of the subsequent annual negotiations over guaranteed sugar prices. However sugar has now been caught up in the same pressures for trade liberalisation that led to the challenge to the Banana Protocol through the WTO, although this has yet to to lead to its final demise.

By contrast the Rum Protocol, examined briefly in Chapter Six, will effectively end in 2003. Here the conflict lay between the traditional ACP producers, particularly the Bahamas and Trinidad and Tobago, and Martinique and Guadeloupe, Overseas Departments of France. However this is one product in which the opening up of the EU market to imports may benefit the ACP producers if they are able to prevent unfair competition from other subsidised international competitors. For the ACP rum exporters the future lies in a shift away from bulk exports towards higher margin branded products.

It is usual at this point to thank those who provided secretarial support in the preparation of this book, however as no such assistance has been forthcoming I must accept responsibility not only for any errors in the content that I have provided, but also in the typesetting.

1 The Lomé Convention and the Commonwealth

STEPHEN DEARDEN

Introduction

By the 1990s the European Community (EC) itself was the world's fifth largest aid donor, responsible for 10.5 per cent of world aid, while the EU, both through the Commission's Development budgets (EC) and the development assistance provided by the Member States, accounted for over 60 per cent of global Official Development Assistance. The European Commission is also responsible for all external trade relationships and is a principal player in determining the trade prospects for developing countries within the World Trade Organisation (WTO) negotiations.

In this chapter I wish to provide an overview of EU trade and aid policy, to chart its evolution and identify its major weaknesses, particularly with reference to the members of the Commonwealth. This is a time of transition in EU development policy. The negotiations for the successor to the current Lomé agreement (Lomé IV) have just been concluded and have been heavily influenced by the ongoing negotiations of the Millennium Round of the WTO. The end of the 'cold war' has dramatically changed the priorities of Western Development Policy and, combined with the emphasis upon 'structural adjustment', 'good governance' and a 'poverty focus' face the governments of many Less Developed Countries (LDC) with a more demanding agenda. It is therefore a particularly opportune moment to take stock of EU development policy.

I will begin by examining trends in EU development assistance and the aid offered under the Lomé Conventions. I will then turn to the trade dimension of Lomé and consider the impact that it has had on the beneficiaries of its trade concessions. The chapter then provides a critical overview of the Conventions and discusses how far Cotonou appears to be addressing these problems.

The Lomé Conventions

The founding Treaty of Rome in 1957, under French insistence, had made provision for aid and trade concessions for those overseas territories with which prospective Member States had special relations. The subsequent 1963 Yaoundé Convention had offered assistance to 18 Less Developed Countries. With the accession of the UK the existing Convention was extended to include most of the LDC that had enjoyed Commonwealth trade preferences, although excluding the larger Asian Commonwealth states (India, Pakistan, Bangladesh). The first Lomé Convention was signed in 1975 and now comprises 71 LDC forming the ACP group (Africa, Caribbean and Pacific) of which 35 are also members of the Commonwealth.[1] Each Convention usually lasted five years, although Lomé IV was extended for ten years until 2000, and has both an aid and trade component.

Aid is provided under Lomé through an associated European Development Fund (EDF); thus Lomé IV has two EDFs (7 and 8) each of five years duration. However funds need not be expended within the period of a particular EDF, and the substantial gap between allocation and disbursement has become a major focus of criticism. Unlike the EU budget, the share for funding the EDF is determined by inter-governmental negotiation. Germany and France are the main contributors, providing about half of the total funding (Table 1.1). The ACPs also have access to funds provided by the European Investment Bank (EIB). Funds are allocated to conventional aid projects (programmable), to Stabex and Sysmin, humanitarian aid and Structural Adjustment Support (SAS). Programmable aid is divided into regional[2] and country shares, with each ACP government then negotiating a National Indicative Programme (NIP), setting out the framework within which funds will be allocated. Stabex offered compensation for falls in revenues arising from instability in the export earnings from 48 agricultural commodities, while Sysmin offered similar compensation for instability in mineral export revenues.

The trade concessions under Lomé offer duty-free access for ACP exports of primary products, but excluding many CAP agricultural products. There are special arrangements for bananas, rum, beef and sugar. Most manufacturers also enter the EU duty-free. Approximately 97 per cent of ACP exports to the EU enter tariff-free.

Table 1.1 EDF Funding

	Per cent		
	Shares of EDF Funding		EDF as per cent of National Aid Budget 1997
	EDF VII (1990-5)	EDF VIII (1995-2000)	
Austria		2.6	31
Belgium	4.0	3.9	43
Denmark	2.1	2.1	9
Finland		1.5	24
France	24.4	24.3	18
Germany	26.0	23.4	36
Greece	1.2	1.2	
Ireland	0.6	0.6	33
Italy	13.0	12.5	135
Luxembourg	0.2	0.3	21
Netherlands	5.6	5.2	12
Portugal	0.9	1.0	37
Spain	5.9	5.8	42
Sweden		2.7	8
UK	16.4	12.7	36

Source: ACP – EC Courier Jan-Feb 1996 & Reisen (1999) p. 105.

EC Aid

EC aid is not only financed through the EDFs but also through the EC's general budget. Over the period 1986-95 56 per cent of EC aid was allocated from the Communities general budget (Cox & Koning 1997), while the EDFs contributed only 37 per cent; down from 52 per cent in the years 1986-89. The remaining funds were provided by the EIB. Although the ACP states have also received some assistance from the EC's general budget, mainly as food aid, this change has reflected a major shift in the ECs aid priorities. Although sub-Saharan Africa continues to be the main recipient of EC aid, its share has fallen from 70 per cent of EC aid in the 1970s to only 40 per cent today. By contrast the share of EC aid received by the countries of Central and Eastern Europe and other states which were formally part of the Soviet Union, has risen to 23 per cent. Asia has been the other region which has seen its share of aid decline, down from a peak of 21 per cent in 1980-81 to 7 per cent today. These general trends are even more starkly illustrated in the experience of particular countries. In 1970-74 India was the largest single recipient of EC aid, at 6.5 per cent, closely followed by Bangladesh (6.4 per cent). Twenty years later Bangladesh was receiving only 1.5 per cent of total aid and India even less.

Between 1986 and 1995 EC aid to the ACP group more than doubled from ECU 1.1bn. to ECU 2.6bn.; of this 80 per cent was received under Lomé.

Table 1.2 ACP Aid

	Million ECU						
	1986	**1988**	**1990**	**1992**	**1994**	**1995**	**1986-1995**
Commitments	1141	2869	1362	2765	3514	2599	23774
per cent Total EC Aid	45	68	42	42	48	35	47
Disbursements	1057	1542	1703	2592	2445	2287	18550
per cent Total EC Aid	63	58	59	55	44	42	51

Source: Cox & Koning.

Sub-Saharan Africa was the principle recipient in this group, taking 76 per cent of committed funds; with Ethiopia, Côte d'Ivoire, Mozambique, Cameroon and Nigeria taking 27 per cent of this total (Table 1.3). Commitments to the Sub-Saharan region have been unstable on an annual basis, principally as a result of problems with an agreement as to Stabex payments in 1993. However disbursements have been more consistent, if always significantly lower, than the committed fund figure. In the Caribbean aid increased significantly from ECU 55m. in 1986 to reach ECU 291m. by 1995. This increase arose from the accession of the Dominican Republic and Haiti under Lomé IV; the two countries accounting for 58 per cent of the regions EC aid in 1995. In the Pacific, Papua New Guinea accounted for 58 per cent of the regions ECU 21m. aid, with the Solomon Islands taking the next largest share at 9 per cent.

Table 1.3 Major Commonwealth Recipients of EC Aid

	Million ECU	
	1991-95	**EDF 8**
Mozambique	547	287
India	462	
Bangladesh	459	
South Africa	457	
Zambia	442	222
Uganda	430	268
Tanzania	414	319
Zimbabwe	375	125
Nigeria	362	
Kenya	330	173
Papua New Guinea	321	50
Malawi	315	203
Ghana	299	154
Pakistan	175	
Jamaica	172	60
Sierra Leone	152	122
Botswana	127	38
Lesotho	125	63
Trinidad &Tobago	99	22
Guyana	87	37
Mauritius	80	45
Cyprus		78
Swaziland	55	41

Source: Eurostat.

Although the sums received by the Caribbean and Pacific are relatively small these states have amongst the highest per capita aid received from the EC.

In terms of the components of EDF funding programmable aid continues to represent the major element (Table 1.4), although it had declined from 66 per cent of EDF 6 to 58 per cent of EDF 8. Within programmable aid, project finance now accounts for less than half of all expenditures, down from two-thirds in the 1980s. The remaining programmable aid is now directed at general ACP budgetary support and rehabilitation of existing infrastructure. The focus of project finance has also changed over time. Whereas Lomé I and II concentrated on industrial development, Lomé III emphasised the development of the rural and agricultural sectors. Thus between 1986 and 1995 most project aid concentrated upon rural development (7 per cent) and agriculture (6 per cent), with transport and communications accounting for 11 per cent, industry, mining and construction 8 per cent and social infrastructure 7 per cent. The regional component of programmable aid has constituted about 9 per cent of programmable funds and is intended to encourage regional co-operation between ACP states.

Of the non-programmable aid components Stabex is the most important. Intended to provide compensation for reductions in agricultural export earnings - mainly cocoa, coffee and cotton - it represents 14 per cent of EDF funding. Although the number of eligible products has been extended over the Çonventions from 29 to 50, the use of the compensation has increasingly been constrained. With Lomé IV the use of the grants must now be agreed between the EC and the ACP country. The main Commonwealth beneficiaries of Stabex include Kenya, Uganda and Papua New Guinea. For the Solomon Islands, Vanuatu and Western Samoa,

Table 1.4 European Development Funds

	Million ECU		
	EDF6	**EDF7**	**EDF8**
Programmed Aid	5053	6251	7562
Stabex/Sysmin	1340	1980	2375
Other Non-Programmed	1260	1790	1630
Structural Adjustment	-	1153	1400
Total	7653	11174	12967

Source: Eurostat.

Stabex represents the largest component of the funds they receive from the EC. It has also been important to St. Lucia and St. Vincent, in particular years, as compensation for falls in banana earnings.

Sysmin provides similar compensation for fluctuations in the earnings from mineral exports. An ACP can request support if mining products account for 15 per cent of their export earnings (10 per cent for Low Income Developing Countries). Under Lomé II and III Sysmin offered only loans, but from Lomé IV these funds are grants. The overall utilisation of these funds has been relatively low. Of the ECU 1.2bn. committed between 1986 and 1995 only ECU 413 m. was disbursed (Cox

& Koning 1997). In part this may reflect the stability of mineral earnings but it has also been criticised as a reflection of the administrative complexities of the operation of this particular policy instrument. Sysmin is important for Zambia and Namibia, with some funding for Guyana, Jamaica and Papua New Guinea.

In 1987 the EC had introduced a Special Debt Programme which was the first instrument to be specifically linked to structural adjustment. But with Lomé IV Structural Adjustment Assistance (SAS) moved centre stage. In the period preceding the negotiations for Lomé IV the LDCs had faced a significant deterioration in their economic prospects. Falling commodity prices, increasing world interest rates and increasing borrowing, had created a serious debt problem. At the same time the end of the 'cold war' was changing the political relationship between the West and Developing world. Consequently the UK and the Netherlands argued strongly for a greater proportion of funds to be allocated specifically to SAS. These funds are intended to encourage the adoption of a reform package seeking to achieve macro stability and export-led growth. To achieve these objectives LDC governments were expected to focus upon de-regulation of markets, privatisation of state-owned enterprises, balancing government budgets, monetary restraint and devaluation. Under the Mid Term Review of Lomé IV further 'encouragement' was offered to ACP governments through the adoption of a two phase release of EC funds; the second 30 per cent being 'performance related'. This formed part of the movement to a rolling programme, with funds released in two year tranches on the basis of implementation of an agreed five year economic programme. Unexpended funds could also be rolled over into the tranche. These changes are intended to provide greater continuity. EDF 7 allocated ECU 1.1bn. and EDF 8, ECU 1.4bn., to SAS (Table 1.1) offering both general budget support and import finance. The major Commonwealth beneficiaries of SAS have been Tanzania, Zambia and Ghana, and in the Caribbean, Jamaica.

Between 1986 and 1995 the ACP states also received concessionary loans worth ECU 2.9 bn. Of this ECU 1.6 bn. was from EIB 'own resources' with interest rates subsidised by the EDFs and ECU 1.3bn. from the EDFs as risk capital. 80 per cent of these loans were received by the Sub-Saharian ACPs with Nigeria alone receiving 15 per cent (ECU 350 m.), Zimbabwe 9 per cent and Kenya 6 per cent. In the Caribbean, Jamaica and Trinidad and Tobago were the major recipients and in the Pacific Papua New Guinea. The largest sector to receive loan finance was industry, mining and construction (26 per cent), followed by energy (23 per cent), transport and communications (11 per cent) and agriculture (11 per cent)

(Cox & Koning 1997).

By 1998 56 per cent of EDF expenditure was project aid, 20 per cent was for SAS, 6 per cent Stabex, 3 per cent Sysmin and 14 per cent and was directed through the EIB.

Trade

The EU maintains a pyramid of trade preferences that ranges from the free-trade for members of the European Economic Area to the Most Favoured Nation (MFN) access of other industrialised countries. 54 LDC obtain access under the General System of Preferences (GSP). Introduced in 1971 this was intended to offer duty-free access for LDC manufactured goods. However it has serious limitations and has excluded higher income LDCs and products that achieve an import penetration of more than 20 per cent (10 per cent for textiles). In 1995 the EU adopted a new ten year GSP expressed as a percentage of the MFN tariff and ranging from 35 per cent to 85 per cent for sensitive products (e.g. footwear, electronics and motor vehicles). There also remains a safeguard clause allowing the reintroduction of duties should the level of imports cause particular difficulties for an EU producer.

For the ACP Lomé offers a significant competitive advantage in the EU market by allowing duty free access for manufactured goods, as well as for primary commodities and most non-CAP agricultural products. Approximately 97 per cent of ACP exports are able to enter the EU duty free. Special regimes exist for bananas, rum, beef and sugar, covering approximately 7 per cent of ACP exports. An important limitation on the value of these concessions has been the rules of origin. Currently 85 per cent of the value of the product must be added in the ACP state for it to be imported duty-free. In return for these concessions the Community only requires that ACP states do not discriminate in their treatment of EU Member States.

ACP Trade Performance

Although the EU is an important market for many Commonwealth states – (Table 1.5) accounting for 80 per cent of Mauritius's export earnings, 73 per cent for Sierra Leone, 75 per cent for Uganda and 70 per cent for St. Lucia - the export performance of the ACP group has been disappointing, despite their Lomé concessions. In 1976 the ACPs exported goods worth

ECU 10.5 bn., giving them 6.7 per cent of total EU imports. By 1994 although the total exports from the expanded ACP group were ECU 18.6 bn., this represented only 3.4 per cent of EU imports. These exports to the EU also continued to be dominated by primary products. 28 per cent of all ACP exports to the EU between 1988 and 1992 were petroleum products and another 30 per cent other primary products. The oil exporter Nigeria is

Table 1.5 ACP Commonwealth Exports to EU 1992

	Million ECU	Per cent EU ACP Imports
Nigeria	3,990	22
Mauritius	833	4.6
Ghana	572	3.2
Kenya	525	2.9
Zimbabwe	514	2.9
Jamaica	282	1.6
Zambia	245	1.4
Bahamas	224	1.2
Papua New Guinea	209	1.2
Malawi	187	1.0
Sierra Leone	184	1.0
Trinidad and Tobago	175	1.0
Tanzania	156	0.9
Namibia	154	0.9
Guyana	149	0.8
Uganda	127	0.7
Swaziland	123	0.7
Fiji	113	0.6
Gambia	98	0.5
St. Lucia	83	0.5
Botswana	83	0.5
St. Vincent	68	0.4
Belize	48	0.3

Total ACP Exports to EU: ECU 17,960,00.
Source: Davenport (1995).

thus the dominant exporter to the EU, accounting for 22 per cent of ACP exports to the EU in 1992. Meanwhile the share of ACPs in EU manufactured imports had fallen from 6.6 per cent in 1962 to only 1.5 per cent in 1987. This performance is poor, even compared with other LDCs. Between 1976 and 1993 the ACP group only managed to increase their processed goods exports by an average of 4.4 per cent per annum; by comparison the non-ACP LDCs averaged 13 per cent per annum (ODI 1995b). However the greatest contrast is with the performance of the Newly Industrialising Countries (NICs). The share of the four Asian NICs - South Korea, Taiwan, Singapore and Hong Kong - had reached 8.6 per cent as early as 1980. By 1995 they were accounting for 85 per cent of all LDC manufactured imports into the EU.

However in the case of certain countries and products there is evidence to suggest that Lomé preferences have made some contribution to their establishment and growth, although not necessarily as the principle factor. The Bahamas and Trinidad and Tobago now derive a third of their EU export earnings from the sale of rum where they enjoyed a 13 per cent tariff advantage. Nigeria has taken 8.6 per cent of the EU market for leather imports and Mauritius exports ECU 19m. (1992) of clocks and watches to the EU, although this has been eroded by the revival of competition from Switzerland.

But the most important concession under Lomé for manufactures is the exemption from the quantitative restrictions of the Multifibre Arrangement (MFA), which particularly inhibits India, Pakistan and Bangladesh. Although Zimbabwe and Jamaica have exploited their MFA exemption, the principle beneficiary has been Mauritius. Diversifying from a dependence on sugar, by 1990 68 per cent of its exports were manufacturers, particularly clothing. However, as McQueen (1990) argues, Lomé concessions in themselves were not the only element in their success. The export orientation of government policy had made Mauritius particularly attractive for foreign investment. Similarly as Zimbabwe removed exchange and import controls in the early 1990s it doubled its manufactured exports - particularly of clothing, textiles and shoes. The EU accounts for 36 per cent of these exports (Riddell 1990). However under the Uruguay Round of GATT the MFA quotas are due to be phased out by 2005, together with a general reduction in tariffs on textiles and clothing of 22 per cent. This will significantly enhance the level of competition faced by ACP exporters from other LDCs, but will benefit Commonwealth Asian producers.

Even in the case of tropical primary products the benefits of the ACP Lomé preferences are not necessarily apparent (Davenport 1988). Thus although the ACP producers gained EU market share from other LDCs in the 1980s in coffee, tobacco and palm oil, where they enjoy preferential access, they also gained share in tea where they have none. However the

ACP have benefited from their competitive advantage in fish exports to the Community. As long as the vessels involved are at least 50 per cent owned by ACP or EU nationals their catch enjoys duty-free access to the EU market. Processed fish products face further rules-of-origin restrictions, but these have been relaxed under Lomé IV. Between 1976-92 ACP fish exports grew 17 per cent annually, compared with 14 per cent from the rest of the world (Davenport et al. 1995). For the Seychelles EU fish exports grew from nothing in 1976 to ECU 17m. in 1992. Frozen fish represented 21 per cent of all ACP fish exports in 1992 and were particularly important for Kenya and Namibia.

However of most importance for some Commonwealth ACPs are the Commodity Protocols attached to the Lomé Convention (see ECDPM 1999b). The Sugar Protocol is a successor to the Commonwealth sugar agreement and is uniquely independent of the Lomé Conventions and therefore of infinite duration. It guarantees purchases of a particular volume of sugar - 1.26m. tons in 1992 - at fixed prices. This quota is currently allocated to 15 ACPs (Table 1.6). As their exports consistently exceed their quotas there is continual pressure to increase them. The Rum Protocol was particularly important to five Caribbean ACPs which account for almost all of EU imports (Table 1.7). The value of their exports has risen significantly, from ECU 21.6m. in 1976 to ECU 249m. in 1998. However under an EU-US deal the EU agreed to phase out the tariff-quota on non-ACP rum from 2000, with the market opening up completely by 2003. A number of ACP states also benefit from the Beef and Veal Protocol that provides a 92 per cent reduction in the variable levy. The quota is shared between Botswana (18,900 tons), Kenya (142 tons), Madagascar (7,579 tons), Swaziland (3,363 tons), Zimbabwe (9,100 tons) and Namibia (13,000 tons). Only Botswana, Namibia and Zimbabwe utilise their quotas to any serious extent and have never exceeded them.

Finally mention must be made of the Banana Protocol. Banana exports are significant to the economies of a number of small Caribbean island economies. In 1993 they represented 41 per cent of the export earnings of St. Lucia, 38 per cent for St. Vincent and 41 per cent for Dominica. With the creation of the single European market an EU regime was required to replace the national trade agreements. The 1993 Banana Protocol allowed for the duty-free access of 875,000 tons of ACP bananas, allocated on a country basis, and 2 m. tons of 'Dollar' and non-traditional ACP bananas under a tariff. 'Dollar' bananas from Latin American plantations have a significant cost advantage and their multi-national company importers challenged the EU before the GATT and subsequently the WTO. This successful challenge has emerged as a major influence in the formulation of the Cotonou Agreement.

Table 1.6 Sugar Protocol

	1992 Quota	'000 tons Exports
Barbados	49.3	52.3
Fiji	163.6	247.8
Guyana	157.7	220.3
Jamaica	118.3	126.2
Madagascar	10	10.3
Malawi	20	24.6
Mauritius	487.2	696.2
Swaziland	116.4	234.6
Tanzania	10	11
Trinidad and Tobago	69	46.2
Congo	10	5.9
Belize	39.4	56.7
St. Kitts-Nevis-Anguilla	14.8	20
Kenya	5	0
Uganda	4	0

Source: Davenport (1995) Table 2.7.

Table 1.7 ACP Rum Exports to EU 1992

	ECU '000
Bahamas	30,291
Barbados	1,515
Guyana	7,838
Jamaica	7,242
Trinidad and Tobago	73,579

Source: Davenport (1995) Table 2.8.

The relative failure of the ACP to expand their share of the EU market has been explained by a number factors. Firstly it must be recognised that Lomé offers a very limited comparative advantage to the ACP over the GSP offered to other LDCs. McQueen and Stevens (1989) estimated that only 7 per cent of ACP exports to the EU enjoyed a margin greater than 5 per cent over other LDCs. Despite the tariff advantage being greater with higher levels of processing the ACPs exports have remained predominantly of primary products, which also have a relatively low price elasticity of demand. But the question remains - why have the ACP failed to diversify into higher levels of processed exports?

The answer lies to a considerable degree in 'supply side factors' - the weaknesses of LDC economies that is at the heart of the development problem. Poor infrastructure, limited human capital, low levels of private investment, under-developed financial institutions, poor macro economic management and public administration have all contributed to the inability of the ACP to fully exploit their opportunities in the EU market. But the operation of the EU's Lomé trade concessions has itself presented obstacles to the ACPs.

Critique of Lomé

The Maastricht and Amsterdam Treaties established four principles upon which EC development policy should be based - Complementarity with the development policies of the Member States; administrative Co-ordination with Member States and between Brussels and the local delegations; Coherence between all Community policies to take into account the EC's development objectives; and Consistency between all the external policies of the EC. It is against these criteria that the EC has been found wanting.

It was not until the Maastricht Treaty (1992) that the EC was given a legal basis for its role in development co-operation. However this is not an exclusive competence and the division of responsibility between the EC and the Member states remains an issue for political negotiation. Consequently it not surprising that the EC has been criticised for its inability to coordinate EC and Member State aid programmes, both in Brussels and at the country level. However many failures clearly arise from the internal administrative systems and structure.

The role of the EDF committee in its control of the funding has reduced the discretion of the local EC delegations and contributed to the low rate of disbursement of funds. Meanwhile the division of responsibilities for EC development policy has also contributed to the Communities weakness. Since 1995 policy responsibilities have been allocated between the Directorate Generals on a geographical basis, with DG8 responsible for Lomé and relations with the ACP states. However the administration of the aid programmes has been made the responsibility of a

Common Service (SCE) since 1998. Similarly responsibility for policy and implementation have been allocated to two separate Commissioners. Further problems have arisen in relation to the EC Humanitarian Office (ECHO) whose role and funding have overlapped with those of the DGs. Created in 1992 to provide emergency relief, in 1994 its budget peaked at ECU 746 m. Underlying these co-ordination problems is the fundamental weakness of limited administrative capacity. The EC's aid budget is similar to that of the US and yet the Commission has a staff less than one-third of the size. Consequently there is a great reliance on the use of consultants; for example, in 1996 40 per cent of staff were externally contracted.

Given these administrative weaknesses it is hardly surprising that delays in the disbursement of EDF funds has been a major source of criticism. Reisen (1999) has estimated that the gap between commitments and payments over the period 1993 to 1999 under the EDFs totalled ECU 25bn.

The move towards a rolling programme and general budget support may well exacerbate these administrative failings. To be successful this approach requires careful planning and monitoring within an environment of close co-operation between the EC and ACP. It is likely to require a far higher degree of decentralisation of decision making to EC delegations in ACP states and the more careful management of the release of funds, tied to the annual review process, so as not to disrupt ACP finances.

For the ACP themselves it is essential that the rolling programme does not overburden their administrations and, more fundamentally, that the criteria for the annual assessments is transparent and consistent. The EC has indicated that the criteria for aid allocation should be a combination of an estimate of need and of performance. Need will be defined by a number of economic and social indicators, but performance criteria is more ambiguous. This will include evidence of commitment to sustainable development, poverty eradication, good governance, the quality of macro economic management and sectoral policies and the effectiveness of the utilisation of EC aid. These criteria are far too broad to avoid the problem of arbitrary and political considerations.

Although the EC's development policy has always had as one of its goals the alleviation of poverty, the adoption of many of its Member States of the OECD/DAC commitment to halve the proportion of those in poverty by 2015, has moved this objective central stage. Lomé has a central weakness in this regard in that it excludes nine of the lowest income developing countries. However even over the history of the Convention it has taken time for the primacy of the economic growth objective, with its assumption of 'trickle down', to be challenged. In a succession of

Resolutions by the EC - on measures to combat poverty (1993) and on women (1995) - the emphasis upon food security aid and the prioritisation of education and health in SAS, have reflected the increasing profile of the 'poverty' objective. But the EC is still in the process of developing poverty focused operational strategies.

The EU's commitments to education and health projects has remained at 2-3 per cent over the 1990s and fundability (recipients' ability to replace their own resources with aid funds) has allowed LDC governments to continue to neglect these sectors (Court of Auditors 1996); although in part this has reflected the need by the ACPs to meet their external debt obligations. But the shift away from project aid to general budgetary support has also reduced the EC's ability to influence the allocation of ACP government resources. A successful budgetary support strategy therefore requires a coherent policy, with agreement between all of an ACP's aid donors and the recipient government on its expenditure priorities. While the EC will need to ensure that its Country Programmes have a clear poverty focus, and that the results are consistently monitored, 'ownership' of development strategies by LDC governments is regarded as essential if poverty reduction targets are to be achieved. The emphasis upon 'good governance' in EU-ACP partnership negotiations and the development of a local capacity to engage local 'civil societies' (i.e. local NGOs), reflects this strategy.

Trade

Increasingly the EU has emphasised the role of trade as the stimulus to economic growth in the ACP and their export performance as a measure of of their achievement of integration into the world economy. However the trade concessions offered under Lomé have also been subject to consistent criticism.

As already mentioned the rules-of-origin have proved a significant problem for the ACP. The EU has been accused of using them as a form of hidden protectionism and of failing to recognise the importance of intra-industry trade and offshore assembly (McQueen 1982). The rules have presented a particular problem for the Caribbean and Pacific ACP States where major investors are likely to come from the US and Japan. McQueen and Stevens (1989) found that the rules-of-origin had frustrated the exports of woven cloth from both Mauritius and Jamaica, whilst the export of fish products presented difficulties for some ACPs that lacked their own fishing fleet. In response to these problems the mid-term review of Lomé IV had increased the non-EU/ACP threshold from 10 per cent to 15 per cent of the value of the product and allowed a regional cumulation of inputs from some LDCs which had a customs union or free trade agreement with an ACP. Cumulation is particularly important to the Caribbean ACPs, allowing the use of inputs from Central America, Colombia, Costa Rica, Cuba and Venezuela. The rules-of-orgin remain more restricted for textiles and clothing.

However derogations from the rules-of-origin can be given where 'the development of existing industries or the creation of new industries justifies them' and last for five years, with the possibility of a further five year extension. But where industries have yet to be established it is difficult to provide supporting evidence. Further derogation procedures have been slow, unclear in their evidence requirements and unpredictable in their outcomes, undermining ACP investment planning (Davenport et al. 1995). A number of Commonwealth ACP industries have been identified as having suffered from these problems, including tuna from Fiji, carpets from Jamaica and clothing from Mauritius (McQueen & Stevens 1989).

The most glaring weakness of EU trade policy has been the continued protectionism of the CAP. Not only has this excluded some efficient ACP producers from the EU market, but the need to dispose of EU agricultural surpluses has led to the dumping of subsidised EU exports on the world market. Such surpluses, provided as food aid, can also undermine attempts to foster domestic production in recipient developing countries. Pressure for reform of the CAP has come both from within the EU and from outside. Its continued high cost, and the additional burden which would arise with the entry of Eastern European states, has combined with pressure from GATT and the WTO. The EU is already committed to reducing export subsidies by 21 per cent under the Uruguay Round of GATT. However reform may have mixed consequences for some ACPs, possibly undermining their preferential access to the EU, and there is concern that any changes will favour large scale producers at the expense of small scale ACP farmers.

Cotonou: A Partnership Agreement

While radical changes in the Lomé Convention had been envisioned by the EU, the new ACP-EU Partnership Agreement, signed in Cotonou, Benin, in June 2000, is little different from its predecessors. It will run for the twenty years from 2000 to 2020, with revision every five years. Aid will continue to be dispersed through five year EDFs.

The major difference is in the trade dimension. The obligations of the EU to the WTO has been a major influence in shaping Cotonou. Although the Lomé Conventions had a waiver from the GATT requirements until 2000, the successful challenge to the Banana Protocol has forced a fundamental rethink. Although the WTO allows preferential access for low income less developing countries (LLDCs), the ACP includes many middle income LDCs which do not qualify. For these States any trade preference must be reciprocal i.e. they must offer duty-free access for EU goods. All 15 Caribbean Countries, except Haiti, fall into this category. To meet this requirement the EU intends to introduce Economic Partnership Agreements (EPA) under Cotonou. These free trade agreements must be concluded for all non-LLDC ACP states by 2008, with a transitional period up to 2020, and will usually be regionally based. Those ACP States which feel unable to participate in an EPA will be offered an alternative trade agreement 'equivalent to the current situation' but 'in compliance with WTO rules'. This is most likely to be inclusion in the less generous Generalised System of Preferences that applies to most non-ACP developing countries and which itself is due for revision in 2004.

For the 39 low income ACP states the EU will offer non-reciprocal duty-free access for most of their products by 2005. Importantly for the Caribbean ACPs the commitment to the Sugar, Beef and Banana Protocols has been maintained. The beef and sugar Protocols will continue until 2007, although the banana Protocol will be amended to meet WTO requirements. But the Rum Protocol is to end, with compensating transitional support until 2008.

The EU has commissioned a number of studies (e.g. McQueen 1999) examining the impact upon six regional groupings of adopting EPAs – i.e. CARICOM (Caribbean), EAC (East Africa), Pacific, SADC (South Africa), UEMOA (West Africa) and UDEAC-CEMAC (Central Africa). Despite varying assumptions these studies fail to demonstrate any significant gains in ACP exports to the EU (see ECDPM 1999a). By contrast the EU will succeed in increasing its exports and may offer significant competition to ACP agricultural and domestic manufacturing products. Any advantages identified with EPAs arises from the more uncertain long run dynamic gains of increased regional integration and higher levels of foreign direct investment.

The EU will however have to secure waivers from the WTO for these arrangements. Achieving WTO compatibility, both within the new Convention and its Commodity Protocols, will now become the major factor shaping future ACP-EU trade relations. It is by no means clear that EPAs in themselves will meet the EU's obligations. Article XXIV of the

TO which authorises free trade areas and customs unions, hem to cover 'substantially all trade' - which raises problems with - and to be completed in a 'reasonable length of time', currently . All WTO members must also approve these arrangements.

In terms of aid, EDF 9, which covers the five years up to 2005, will total €13.5bn., a 5 per cent increase on EDF 8. Of this €1.3bn. will be allocated to regional programmes and €2.2bn. to a new Investment Facility. This, together with an additional €1.7bn. of loan funding, will be administered by the European Investment Bank (EIB). This additional funding for investment is particularly intended to support the private sector, which will now have access to EIB loans without requiring State guarantees. Undisbersed sums from previous Conventions, totalling approximately €10bn., will also be added to EDF 9, producing a global sum of €24bn. available for the period 2000-2007. Aid instruments are to be rationalised with an emphasis upon a rolling programme of general budgetary support and sectoral programmes. The EU has also committed itself to carry out a major reform of its aid administration in order to improve the rate of payment of the funds. It is hoped that such disbursements may reach €3.5bn. per annum after these changes.

To compensate for the erosion of their preferences under the various Commodity Protocols, the EU will offer additional financial support to those ACP industries affected so as to attempt to maintain their competitiveness.

Meanwhile a new system of compensation for reductions in export earnings, to replace Sysmin and Stabex, has been introduced. Under Lomé IV these two instruments had increasingly been focused upon sectoral structural reforms rather than income support. The use of these funds for diversification had ended the link with producer compensation. However these instruments were seen as poorly adapted to this wider role. The preparation of ad hoc programmes, compatible with the NIPs, resulted in administrative duplication and Stabex and Sysmin funding was, by its nature, unpredictable. Under the new scheme any ACP will qualify for support if it experiences a 10 per cent fall in earnings (2 per cent for low income countries) from a good or from total agricultural or mining earnings (provided that they represent at least 40 per cent of a countries exports) and this results in a 10 per cent increase in the public sector deficit. At the start of each EDF all ACPs will be allocated a financial envelope, in addition to their NIP, to meet the costs of this support, should they qualify, thereby enhancing the countries financial planning. Those states particularly dependent upon mining or agricultural exports and the low-income, land locked and island economies, will receive more generous funding. Subject to joint agreement, this finance can be used to sustain the NIP in the face of unexpected fiscal shocks or it may be allocated to specific sectors. A review mechanism will also be established to ensure that sufficient funds are available to any ACP to ensure that there is adequate on-going finance to sustain the compensation scheme for any individual state.

Another innovation in the new Agreement is the change to a more flexible criteria for the assessment of each country's needs and performance for aid allocation. Country performance in implementing institutional reforms, in allocating resources and in macro management will be assessed in an undefined but 'objective and transparent manner', while spending programmes will contain jointly-agreed review criteria.

The new agreement also includes a significant political dimension recognising the need for a broad political dialogue beyond development issues. For the Caribbean States the most pertinent issues are likely to be those of immigration and drugs. Whilst emphasising 'dialogue' between the EU and ACP governments there is a strong emphasis upon ACP obligations to observe 'essential elements' - respect for human rights, democratic government and the rule of law. After objections from the ACPs, 'good governance' is regarded as a 'fundamental' element and breaches are subject to less rigorous sanctions. However even here serious cases of corruption can lead to the suspension of aid, although only after a process of consultation. It is unlikely that these requirements will present serious difficulties for most of the Commonwealth Caribbean States. What however is becoming more problematic for these countries is the pressure from the G7 and OECD on offshore tax havens, partly driven by concern about money laundering. Hosting offshore financial centres is an important source of revenues for many of the Caribbean island economies. There is the danger that the 'good governance' and 'rule of law' clauses of Cotonou could in the future be employed to ensure conformity with OECD requirements.

Beyond the encouragement of the private sector Cotonou also emphasises the future role of 'civil society' - i.e. local non-governmental organisations and local authorities. They are to be consulted in the formulation of development strategies, involved in the delivery of local projects and provided with support to increase their organisational capacity. Their role is seen as crucial in achieving the primary objective of poverty reduction and central to the more pluralistic and devolved approach advocated in the new Agreement.

From the perspective of the Caribbean ACPs there was much to be welcomed in the Cotonou Agreement. The special needs of the island

ACPs is recognised throughout the Agreement. Their general vulnerability is acknowledged in Article 2, while Art. 32.2, addressing environmental and natural resource issues, requires co-operation to take account of their particular problems and the threat posed by climate change. Art. 35.3 calls for their special treatment in economic and trade co-operation and Art. 56.2 in development finance. Art. 68.3 asserts that in the allocation of compensation for fluctuations in export earnings 'the least developed, landlocked and island ACP states shall receive more favourable treatment'. Finally Art. 84 calls for special attention to be paid to these states in regard to 'the strengthening of regional co-operation, transport and communications infrastructure, the efficient exploitation of marine resources..., structural adjustment..., and the implementation of food management strategies and integrated development programmes'.

Throughout the Agreement there is an emphasis upon regional co-operation, with an expectation on the part of the EU that non-LDCs will move to EPAs from 2008. However these are only described in broad terms and the Agreement still states that 'the Parties reaffirm their attachment to ensuring special and differential treatment for all ACP countries' (Art. 35.3) in both economic and trade co-operation. Thus the possibility remains of alternative trade arrangements, tailored to the needs of individual ACP States. The ACPs therefore have considerable scope for negotiation over the coming years, especially within the context of the current WTO round where further significant changes may occur. Already the EU has offered tariff and quota free access to the EU market to all 48 low-income developing countries, with the exception of arms and ammunition (known as EBA - Everything But Arms). For sensitive products, including bananas and sugar, there would be a three year phase-in. However this would only include the 39 low-income ACP countries, none of whom are Commonwealth Caribbean states. Thus they will face enhanced competition from an additional nine low-income developing counties.

The need for change had already been recognised by the Caribbean ACPs themselves, as the successive GATT rounds and the extension of EU Association Agreements had eroded the value of the ACP preferences. The concessions most of value remain the commodity Protocols and the exemption from the export restrictions of the Multifibre Arrangement affecting textiles and clothing. Even the Protocols that survive the demands of the WTO are likely to become less significant as the EU reduces guaranteed prices under Common Agricultural Policy reforms. Meanwhile the quantitative restrictions of the Multifibre Arrangement will be phased out by 2005 under existing EU commitments to the WTO.

Cotonou places considerable emphasis upon the need for 'capacity building' in the transitional period between 2002 and 2008. To achieve this the Caribbean ACPs will be building upon the development policies that they have been pursuing for many years, as outlined in Chapter 2. These have focused upon investment in physical infrastructure and human capital. Raising the overall educational and skills levels of their populations, particularly to meet the needs of the growing service sectors, is clearly recognised. Development of the tourism industry is seen as particularly important to the diversification of the Caribbean economies, and this is specifically recognised in the Agreement. The €2bn. Investment Facility is regarded as central to the expansion of this and other new export sectors, especially in the face of a likely decline in other forms of development assistance. The Investment Facility can fund new enterprises or joint-ventures in non traditional industries, provide equity finance and attract co-financing from other sources of international finance. It is regarded as the essential source of funding for the private sector to complement the infrastructure development role of the public sector. For the small States of the Caribbean these funds are likely to be made available through regional financial institutions.

Thus there is much to play for in the new Agreement. Many important issues remain unresolved, especially in regard to trade and the detailed implementation of the new rolling programme of general budgetary support. Unlike the African ACPs most of the Commonwealth Caribbean States have a history of reasonable economic success, despite the particular vulnerabilities of being island economies. The challenge will lie in their ability to fully exploit the opportunities that the new Agreement offers and to avoid being marginalised in the EU development debate, which is increasingly dominated by Africa and the demands of the more politically sensitive border States of Central/Eastern Europe and the Mediterranean.

Notes

1. Angola, Antigua*, Bahamas*, Barbados*, Belize*, Benin, Botswana*, Burkina Faso, Burundi, Cameron, Cape Verde, Central African Republic, Chad, Comoros, Congo, Côte d'Ivoire, Djibouti, Dominica*, Dominican Republic, Equatorial Guinea, Eritrea, Ethiopia, Fiji*, Gabon, Gambia*, Ghana*, Grenada*, Guinea, Guinea Bissau, Guyana*, Haiti, Jamaica*, Kenya*, Kiribati*, Lesotho*, Liberia, Madagascar, Malawi*, Mali, Mauritius*, Mauritania, Mozambique*, Namibia*, Niger, Nigeria*, Papua New Guinea*, Rwanda, Sao Tome, Senegal, Seychelles*, Sierra Leone*, Solomon Islands*, South Africa*, St. Kitts*, St. Vincent*, St. Lucia*, Somalia, Sudan, Suriname, Swaziland*, Tanzania*, Togo, Tonga*, Trinidad and Tobago*, Tuvalu*, Uganda*, Vanuatu*, Western Samoa*, Zaire, Zambia*, Zimbabwe*. *Commonweath members.

2. ACP Regions - Sahelian & Coastal West Africa; Central Africa: Horn of Africa & East Africa; Southern Africa; Indian Ocean; Caribbean; Pacific.

References

Cox A. & Koning A. (1997), *Understanding European Community Aid*, Overseas Development Institute, London.

Davenport M. (1988), European Community Barriers to Tropical Products: Working paper 27, Overseas Development Institute, London.

Davenport M., Hewitt A. & Koning A. (1995), *Europe's Preferred Partners? The Lomé Countries in World Trade*: Overseas Development Institute, London.

ECDPM (1999a), The EC's Impact Studies on Regional Economic Partnership Agreements: Lomé Negotiating Brief No. 5.

ECDPM (1999b), The Future of Lomé's Commodity Protocols: Fiddling while Rum Burns?: Lomé Negotiating Brief No. 6.

European Commission (1997), Green Paper on Relations between the EU and the ACP Countries on the Eve of the 21st Century.

European Commission (1999), EU-ACP Cooperation in 1998.

European Court of Auditors 1996. Annual Report 1995, Official Journal of the European Communities.

Faber G. & Roelfsema H. (1997), The Lomé Convention and Development in Sub-Saharan Africa: *European Foreign Affairs Review 2*, pp. 367-386.

McQueen M. (1982), Lomé and the Protective Effects of Rules of Origin: *Journal of World Trade Law*, pp. 119-132.

McQueen M. (1990), ACP Export Diversification: The Case of Mauritius : ODI Working Paper No. 41.

McQueen M. (1999), The Impact Studies on the Effects of REPAs between the ACP and the EU: University of Reading.

McQueen M. & Stevens C. (1989), Trade Preferences and Lomé IV, Non-Traditional ACP Exports to the EC: *Development Policy Review 7* (3) pp. 239-60.

Overseas Development Institute (1995), EU Aid post-Maastricht: Fifteen in to One?, Briefing Paper 2, April.

Overseas Development Institute (1995b), The Impact of the Uruguay Round on ACP Manufactured Products. Final Report for UNIDO.

Reisen Mirjam van (1999), *EU Global Player: The North South Policy of the EU*, International Books, Utrecht.

Riddell R. (1990), ACP Export Diversification: The Case of Zimbabawe: ODI Working Paper No. 38.

Stevens C. (1990), ACP Export Diversification: The Case of Jamaica, Kenya and Ethiopia: ODI Working Paper No. 40.

2 European Union Aid

STEPHEN DEARDEN

There are fifteen ACP states in the Caribbean region, seven Overseas Territories (OCT) of the UK and the Netherlands and three Overseas Departments of France (DOM). These 25 territories have a combined population of 22 million and an average GNP of $4500 (1998), although this disguises considerable variation. Since 1975 the EU has provided aid worth ECU 1,785m. to the region co-ordinated through the Caribbean Forum.

In this chapter I will be concentrating upon three groups of Commonwealth States - Belize and Guyana; the larger island economies of Jamaica, Barbados, the Bahamas and Trinidad and Tobago; and the fifteen smaller island economies of the region, including the British Overseas Territories (OCT) (see Tables 2.1 and 2.2).

The states share many characteristics in common. Belize and Guyana, because of their geographical position, are isolated from world markets and share the transport problems of the island economies. Many of these countries have few natural resources and all are vulnerable to recurrent hurricanes. With the exception of the larger economies of Jamaica and Trinidad and Tobago, these States have little manufacturing, and that which does exist is concentrated upon the processing of primary products (e.g. alcoholic drinks), garments, footwear and furniture. Their economies are relatively open, with export/GNP ratios in the range of 50 per cent to 90 per cent. They are particularly dependent upon the export of a limited range of primary products, especially bananas and sugar, although tourism is becoming an important focus of economic activity. Fluctuations in the price or volume of commodity exports has a major impact upon their foreign exchange earnings, which, combined with their dependence upon imports of manufactures, fuel and food, can have a major disruptive effect upon their economies. Thus although they have a relatively high GNP per capita, compared with other developing countries, they experience greater economic instability (Commonwealth Secretariat 1997).

Table 2.1 The Commonwealth Caribbean

	1999 Population '000	1999 GNP per cap. $	Growth % 1989-99	1999 Current Account $m.	1998 Debt $m.
Antigua & Barbuda	70	8990	3.1	-98	467
Bahamas	300	11510	-0.4	-594	n.a
Barbados	270	8620	1.3	-131	644
Belize	250	2730	4.1	-58	338
Dominica	70	3170	1.9	-30	109
Grenada	100	3450	2.6	-104	183
Guyana	860	740	5.7	75	1688
Jamaica	2600	2530	0.6	-326	3995
St. Kitts & Nevis	40	6420	4.3	-78	115
St. Lucia	150	3770	3.6	-54	184
St. Vincent & the Grenadines	110	270	3.3	-71	168
Trinidad & Tobago	1300	4750	2.4	13	2193

Average - $4949.
Source: World Bank.

Table 2.2 The Overseas Territories

	1992 Population	1992 GNP per capita $
Anguilla	9000	6834
British Virgin Islands	16750	10880
Cayman Islands	26000	18520
Montserrat	11395	5976
Turks & Caicos Islands	14000	6252

Source: Development, EU 1995.

In the 1980s most of the Commonwealth Caribbean managed to achieve relatively high rates of growth (5 per cent to 6 per cent per annum). This arose from the high levels of aid funding public infrastructure investment, the buoyancy of banana exports and the growth of tourism. But in the early 1990s external aid flows fell (from 9 per cent GDP to 4 per cent GDP) and banana earnings declined. As a result the growth rate halved to 2 per cent to 3 per cent per annum. But expansion in tourism and other services fuelled a recovery later in the 1990s.

Their economic vulnerability arising from their small domestic markets, geographical isolation and dependence on primary exports, has been recognised under the Lomé agreements. Lomé IV emphasises that cooperation with land-locked and island states should be 'aimed at devising and encouraging specific operations to deal with development problems caused by their geographical situations' (Art. 8). Similarly the chapters on agricultural and industrial development call for special attention to be paid to the needs of 'least-developed, land-locked and island ACP states to utilise fully the provisions' (Arts. 52, 97). Although no special fund has been created focused upon the needs of this group of ACP countries, the per capita aid receipts of the Caribbean region have exceeded what can be justified by their relative per capita incomes. This generosity in NIP and regional programme funding is likely to continue under the Cotonou Agreement, especially in the context of the loss of preferences with the erosion of the Commodity Protocols. As we will see, faced with growing trade and budget deficits, falling growth and increasing external debt, the EU has supported Structural Adjustment Programmes and drawings from the Structural Adjustment Facility of Lomé IV.

EU Trade Provisions

The EU is the Caribbean's main export market. In 1997 the Caribbean ACP States, Overseas Departments of France (DOM) and OCTs exported $3,137 m. of goods and services to the EU and imported $3,806 m (Table 2.3). The ACPs benefit from trade preferences with the EU under the Lomé Convention. It allows duty-free access for most ACP exports with special arrangements for bananas, sugar, rum and rice. The EU's Banana Regime, which offers a tariff-quota for traditional ACP banana suppliers, is particularly important for Dominica, Grenada, Jamaica, St. Lucia and St. Vincent, as well as Belize and Suriname. Similarly the Sugar Protocol guarantees limited purchases at a fixed price - the main beneficiaries being Jamaica and Guyana - and Rum may enter duty-free - benefiting the DOMs, Trinidad and Tobago, Jamaica, the Bahamas and Barbados.

Table 2.3 EU-ACP Trade

	ECU Million			
	1997		1998	
	Exports to EU	EU Imports	Exports to EU	EU Imports
Antigua & Barbuda	37	179	10	168
Bahamas	321	592	322	866
Barbados	50	101	54	123
Belize	83	44	97	36
Dominica	33	27	28	29
Grenada	8	15	10	19
Guyana	190	79	159	71
Jamaica	462	310	519	301
St.Kitts & Nevis	14	18	11	25
St.Lucia	51	36	58	38
St.Vincent & the Grenadines	103	54	69	71
Trinidad & Tobago	436	419	377	395

Source: Eurostat.

EU Aid

For the ACPs and OCTs aid is mainly provided through Lomé's associated European Development Funds (EDF) and the resources of the European Investment Bank (Table 2.4). 92 per cent of EDF 8 (1995-2000) was in the form of grants and the largest proportion (44 per cent) was allocated according to the priorities of the national development programmes (NIP) of the ACPs. The NIPs are agreed in consultations between the individual ACPs and the European Commission.

The small scale of many of the island economies has encouraged regional integration, a process encouraged by the EU. As early as 1973 the

Table 2.4 The Value of EU Aid

	ECU Million	
	1986-90	**1991-95**
National Programmes	186.5	292.7
Regional Programmes	78.6	96.1
EIB Loans	133	110.5
Interest rate subsidies	10.6	6.2
Stabex	3.7	43.9
Sysmin	-	23
Structural Adjustment	-	36.7
Food aid/other	53.9	55.2
Total	461.9	668.7

Source: Development June 1995, European Commission.

Caribbean Community (CARICOM) had been formed to promote economic integration, coordinate foreign policy and provide joint services. Thus EU funds are also allocated to regional projects co-ordinated by CARIFORUM (CARICOM plus Haiti, the Dominican Republic and Suriname) with a focus upon economic integration and sustainable development. In 1991-95 ECU 6.1m. was also available for the OCT regional programme which was sometimes used to co-finance ACP regional projects. Of the Lomé IV regional programme 25 per cent was allocated to human resource development, 27 per cent to trade and tourism projects, 25 per cent to agricultural and rural development, 14 per cent to environmental programmes and 7 per cent to transport and communications. Under EDF 8 these regional programmes are to receive ECU 96m. The third largest category of aid is given under Stabex and Sysmin (ECU 67m.) This provides compensation for fluctuations in the export earnings of agricultural and mining products respectively.

Human resource development is regarded as essential in all projects and sectoral programmes and is a particularly high priority in the agricultural sector. Substantial funds have been directed to the regional University of the West Indies. Given the openness of the Caribbean economies significant funds have also been allocated to fostering trade both externally and within the region. The EU has funded a project aimed at enhancing the Caribbean Common Market (CARICOM), including the development of trade information and market advisory services. It has also fostered the creation of the Eastern Caribbean States Export Development Agency based in Dominica. Since 1990 this Agency has launched trade missions to Canada, the US and Puerto Rico and sought to identify experienced export companies. The EU has also been instrumental in establishing a common system for the collection and processing of trade statistics in the Eastern Caribbean (ASYCUDA).

Given the importance of tourism and its perceived potential, this sector has also received substantial EU support. Funds from Lomé III have financed two large programmes. ECU 9m. was used to establish a Caribbean Tourism Development Programme that provided short term consultancies for product development, joint market development with the European travel industry, market research, short training courses and linkage development (use of locally supplied inputs). The second programme (ECU 3m.) provided similar support for tourism development centred upon the Eastern Caribbean States.

The dominance of primary exports in most Caribbean island economies has also led to an emphasise upon agricultural development in the regional programmes. Earlier EDF funding concentrated upon agricultural research, including ECU 5.3m. to the Caribbean Agricultural Research and Development Institute for the local application of research to local husbandry needs, and ECU 2.2m. to the establishment of an international cocoa gene bank. The EU has also supported research into the prevention of Moko disease that affects banana crops. EDF 7 has focused upon agricultural diversification with the provision of credit for small farmers, improvement of international market intelligence and support to the livestock and aquaculture sectors.

The EU has also provided support for a number of transport infrastructure projects. Air transport is crucial for inter-island communication and central to the development of the tourist industry in some countries. Thus the EU has expended ECU 18.5m. on the establishment of an airport on Bequia in the Grenadines and ECU 5.9m. on support for the Leeward Islands Air Transport Corporation to provide technical training. The EU provided a special loan of ECU 5.9m. to the West Indies Shipping Corporation for the purchase of two cargo vessels to provide an enhanced inter-island scheduled service.

Given the dependence of many island economies on the export of a limited number of agricultural products, which are often vulnerable to hurricanes, they have made particular use of the EU's Stabex funds. These provide compensation for serious losses of export earnings arising from price instability or falls in the volume of exports. Compensation has been paid for losses on the export of bananas, cocoa, coconuts, nutmeg, coffee, essential oils and mace, benefiting Grenada, Dominica, St. Lucia and St. Vincent in particular.

The European Investment bank has provided risk capital to the private sector at concessionary rates and project loans, especially in the energy sector, at commercial rates. Over ECU 400m. has so far been lent to the region.

Additional funds have also been made available for those ACP countries undertaking structural adjustment programmes (ECU 37m. EDF 8), including Dominica and Grenada. These grants finance general or sectoral imports and provide technical assistance. The counterpart funds generated from the sale of imports are allocated to financing social programmes such as education and health. The EU also provides some development assistance from its general budget to cover food aid and co-financing of NGO projects.

Continental America

Belize

Belize lies on the Caribbean coast of Central America but is a member of CARICOM. Its economy is dominated by agriculture, fisheries and tourism. GNP per capita at $2,730 is below the Commonwealth Caribbean average of $4,948 (1999) (Table 2.1). The economy is constrained by the small size of the local market, the shortage of qualified manpower and the lack of indigenous energy sources. But over the decade 1989-99 the economy achieved a growth rate of 4.1 per cent. In 1999 of the total exports of $208m. sugar was the largest item ($41m.) followed by bananas ($27m.) and manufactures ($20m.). Imports totaled $366m. Sugar and bananas accounted for 28 per cent and 25 per cent respectively of exports to the EU, which accounts for 44 per cent of Belize's exports and with which it usually runs a trade surplus (Table 2.3). Outstanding debt totalled $361m., with debt servicing of $42m. in 1999. The government ran a budget deficit of 2.6 per cent GDP.

Table 2.5 EU Aid - Country Allocations

	EDF 7				
	NIP	**EIB**	**Total ECU million**	**EDF 1-7 $m**	**1990-97**
<u>ACP</u>					
Antigua & Barbuda	3.5	1	4.5	16.9	21
Bahamas	3.5	0	3.5	34.4	4
Barbados	3.5	10	15.5	53	30
Belize	9	2.5	11.5	40.02	82
Dominica	5.5	2.5	18.7	49	102
Grenada	4.5	1	11.6	41.1	52
Guyana	26	5	39.1	143.9	364
Jamaica	48.5	29	77.5	246.9	389
St. Kitts & Nevis	2.5	3	5.5	20.2	19
St. Lucia	5	3.5	13	38.9	140
St. Vincent & the Grenadines	5	1.5	12	53.4	85
Trinidad & Tobago	17	38	68.1	170.4	86

Sources: OECD, Eurostat.

The public investment programme is mainly funded by external aid. Between 1990 and 1997 Belize received a total of $82m. in EU aid (Table 2.5). Lomé's I to III totaled ECU 32 m. and were focused upon the development of the health sector, both village primary care and the construction of the new Belize City Hospital (ECU 12m.). The other major project begun under Lomé III was the improvement of the Hummingbird Highway joining the Capital with the southern part of the country. EDF 7 allocated a further ECU 9m. to these two projects. Other smaller grants were allocated to micro-credit schemes, refugee settlement, secondary education and veterinary services. From 1993 to 1996 Belize also received ECU 3.3m. under the EU's special assistance programme for traditional banana producers. The European Investment Bank (EIB) has supported projects undertaken by Belize Electricity and the Development Finance Corporation (ECU 6m.).

Under EDF 8 Belize received ECU 9.5m., 53 per cent of which is earmarked for continuation of the two major infrastructure projects. 45 per cent of the National Indicative Programme (NIP) funds are to be applied to 'the development of human and natural resources'. This includes contributions to the Social Investment Fund, improving management of national nature reserves and historical sites - for the development of eco-tourism - micro enterprise development and improvement of public sector financial management and development planning. The EIB has allocated ECU 2.5m. for further investment in the country.

Guyana

Although situated on the South American continent Guyana is historically and politically regarded as part of the Caribbean, indeed it is the home of CARICOMs Secretariat. The economy is dominated by three sectors - the production of rice, sugar and bauxite. Throughout the 70s and 80s mismanagement resulted in the deterioration of these industries and a general economic decline. A long recession and deteriorating balance of payments culminated in $1.6bn. of accumulated foreign debt by 1990. Structural adjustment began at the end of the 80s with the support of the IMF. The economy recovered with 7 per cent growth in 1991 and for the first time in many years Guyana fulfilled its EU sugar quota of 174,000 tons. Guyana sustained this improvement and averaged a growth rate of 5.7 per cent over the decade 1989-99.

By 1998 sugar exports to the EU totaled 193,800 tons, worth ECU 99m. and rice exports ECU 28m. Guyana also benefited from the Rum Protocol, exports of which to the EU were worth $14.2m. in 1992. However outstanding external debt still stands at $1.7bn., there is a balance of payments current account deficit of $75m., inflation is running at 7.5 per cent and the government has a budget deficit of 4.9 per cent of GDP. GNP per capita is by far the lowest in the Caribbean at $740.

Guyana has been one of the major recipients of EU aid in the Caribbean. Between 1990 and 1997 alone it received $364m. Under Lomé I to III ECU 49.5m. of funds were allocated to restoring the neglected infrastructure, including ferries, ports and water supplies. The EIB provided loans of ECU 11.2m. to the private sector. Guyana has also been a major beneficiary of Sysmin funds. ECU 34.5m. was made available to assist in the rehabilitation of the bauxite industry. Most of the ECU 26m. NIP of EDF 7 was employed to restore sea defences, the Demerara

Harbour Bridge and New Amsterdam's water supply and ECU 6.5m. was made available for general import assistance. EDF 8 continued to fund these schemes. Of the ECU 32m. NIP, ECU 4.5m. is funding the water scheme, ECU 8.4m. Demerara bridge and ECU 6.5m. water supply in Pouderoyen. Further substantial work on the sea defences is also continuing. The EU is also providing Structural Adjustment Support (SAS) of ECU 5.3m.

The Larger Island Economies

Barbados

This relatively large economy (GNP $2.3bn.), with a highly educated labour force, is dominated by off-shore finance and tourism, accounting for 72 per cent of GDP. Sugar and rum production are the principal agricultural products. Although the GNP per capita is relatively high for this region ($8,620) Barbados suffered from a severe recession in the early 90s. The sugar industry, one of the major industries of the economy, became bankrupt in 1992. The government undertook major structural adjustment, with the support of the IMF, resulting in a substantial increase in unemployment. By 1998 the economy had recovered and grew at 4.4 per cent, although this fell back to 2.5 per cent in 1999. Over the whole period 1989-99 growth averaged 1.3 per cent. The current account, balanced in 1989, is now in deficit at $131m. Sugar accounts for 11.4 per cent of the total visible exports of $245m., and textiles 11 per cent. Agricultural exports to the EU were worth ECU 32m. in 1998 and industrial products ECU 22m. The EU provides the largest market for Barbados sugar exports, with a quota of 50,312 tonnes. External debt stands at $608m. and the government continues to run a budget deficit equal to 1.4 per cent GDP.

Despite being one of the larger Caribbean island economies Barbados has received relatively limited EU aid. For EDFs 1 to 7 this totaled only ECU 53m. and two-thirds of this was provided as loans or risk capital by the EIB. It has been applied to a wide variety of projects. In agriculture it has funded livestock development (ECU 1m. plus ECU 1.4m. loan) aimed at reducing imports. It includes technical assistance, marketing support and credit for 400 livestock farmers. Similarly a National Fruit Orchard project aims to improve cultivation and provide credit. In the important fisheries industry three schemes for infrastructure improvement have been supported - Oistins, Consett and Skeets Bay. The latter two projects, to improve landing transport and storage, were allocated ECU

1.6m. under EDF 8. The tourism sector has also received EU support through the funding of the 'Barbados Hospitality Institute', a training hotel attached to the Barbados Community College. In terms of general social infrastructure Lomé I has assisted in the upgrading of health care.

EDF 8 has allocated 60 per cent of its funds to human resource development - including a Language Training Centre and support for additional training for public sector administrators - and 13 per cent to the development of manufacturing and services in support of the governments evolving industrial strategy. This continues earlier support for the Barbados Investment and Development Corporation, which has a particular role in marketing rum exports. A further 20 per cent of the NIP has been earmarked for the construction of a forensic laboratory as part of the anti-drugs programme. This will provide a regional facility and forms part of the EU's general support for anti-drugs policies in the Caribbean.

The EIB will provide ECU 10m. under EDF 8. It has previously provided assistance to the Barbados Development Bank, the Central Bank Industrial Credit Fund and support to small and medium sized businesses. The EIB has also part funded the installation of container-handling facilities at Bridgetown Port, upgrading of the power supply and sewage treatment.

The Bahamas

The Bahamas are a group of 700 islands but 75 per cent of the population is located upon only two - New Providence and Grand Bahama. Low levels of economic development on the remaining islands has resulted in a continued shift of population to the main islands. The economy is dominated by tourism, which exploits the islands proximity to the United States. It provides 52 per cent of employment, contributes 65 per cent to GDP and sustains a high GNP per capita ($11,510, 1990). However this sector has failed to maintain its growth in recent years. Offshore banking and finance is also an important part of the economy. Over the years 1989-99 the economy failed to grow. In 1998 the government was running a small deficit, equal to 1.9 per cent GDP, and there was a current account deficit of $594m., but inflation was low at 1.3 per cent.

The government has sought to diversify the economy and reduce the imbalance in development between the larger and smaller islands of the Family Islands group. Under Lomé I and II aid funded an animal feed plant, fruit crop nursery and credit for small enterprises. Lomé III concentrated its funding upon strengthening the electricity supply in the Family Islands and road improvements on Grand Abaco. Total aid under

Lomé I to III totalled ECU 7.9m. Under EDF 7 the ECU 4.4m. NIP funds were allocated to the rehabilitation of a highway on Long Island and two island airports. EDF 8 continues the emphasis upon the development of the Family Islands infrastructure, allocating the ECU 4.5m. of NIP funds to two projects. The EIB has also committed ECU 51.6m. since Lomé I to support the improvement of the electricity and water supplies. The Bahamas have also received regional funds to support the Caribbean Regional Hotel Training Programme based at the Bahamas Hotel Training College.

Jamaica

With a GNP of $6.6bn. Jamaica is the largest economy in the Commonwealth Caribbean. However its large urbanised population of 2.6m. results in a GNP per capita of only $2,600, the lowest apart from Guyana. Agriculture accounts for only 6.9 per cent GNP, manufacturing 12.4 per cent and services, mainly tourism, 65 per cent. Bauxite mining is a major industry. The economy performed well in the 60s and 70s but was hit hard by the oil crisis and the subsequent world recession. This reduced the number of tourists as well as increasing the oil import bill. The government adopted structural reform measures, but the economy recovered only slowly, with growth averaging 1.2 per cent throughout the 80s. Despite an improvement in export performance, in 1995 a loss of foreign exchange reserves led to a depreciation of the currency, with a consequent increase in the rate of inflation, caused the government to adopt a deflationary stance. A tight monetary policy, with an accompanying credit squeeze, and severe drought affecting agriculture, reduced inflation (6 per cent 1998) but caused a contraction in the economy. Thus between 1989-99 the economy only grew by an average of 0.6 per cent per annum.

Tourism now accounts for one-third of foreign exchange earnings, having overtaken bauxite, although this continues to represent 43 per cent of Jamaica's exports to the EU. Jamaica benefits from the Banana, Sugar and Rum Protocols of the EU. In 1999 sugar exports to the EU were worth ECU 80m. (15 per cent EU export earnings), bananas ECU 50m. (10 per cent) and rum ECU 9.5m. (2 per cent). However the current account remains in deficit at $326m. (1999).

The government is continuing with its economic reform package. It has recently eliminated exchange controls, liberalised the economy, introduced a 12.5 per cent consumption tax, reformed the tax system and reduced expenditure upon social services and education. This structural reform package has been supported by an IMF Extended Fund Facility.

However high interest rates continue to inhibit private sector investment. In 1998 the economy contracted 0.5 per cent and stagnated in 1999, meanwhile it is estimated that one-third of the population are living below the poverty line. The external debt burden has risen from $1.7bn. in 1979 to $4.1bn. in 1999.

As would be expected Jamaica has been the largest recipient of EU aid in the Commonwealth Caribbean ($389m.). Under Lomés I to III ECU 87m. was allocated to rural development and infrastructure improvement. Schemes included help for small coffee producers, goat and sheep producers and beekeepers. ECU 7.1m. was provided for improvements at Sangster International Airport and ECU 40m. for sewage improvements at the major tourist resorts. EDF 7 is funding a NIP of ECU 48m. and continues the broad focus upon rural development, infrastructure and the environment. ECU 13.5m. has been allocated to 140 miles of rural road improvements. Technical assistance was also provided to the Ministry of Works and the Water Commission. A major agricultural improvement scheme is also being supported in Eastern Jamaica. Aid was provided under SAS (ECU 2.5m.) and from the NIP (ECU 4.6m.) to fund EU and ACP imports. Sysmin also contributed ECU 25m. in 1994 towards economic diversification.

The NIP under EDF 8 totals ECU 60m. and concentrates on poverty alleviation (65 per cent) and infrastructure. Support was provided to the Jamaica Social Investment Fund, for small and micro-enterprises and local micro projects. Further funds were directed to rural water supply improvements, urban and rural health projects and an East Jamaica Agricultural Development Project. The infrastructure expenditure is also funding rehabilitation of the North Coast Highway, with additional finance from Sysmin. Jamaica has also benefited from a ECU 10.8m. investment in its banana industry, to improve its competitiveness, under the special assistance scheme for traditional EU banana suppliers. To improve the country's general export performance the Jamaican government has already implemented a 'Target Europe Programme' to encourage trade and investment links with the EU. This has also received support under EDF 8.

The EIB has provided ECU 30m. of loans and ECU 5m. in equity participation in small and medium sized firms, ECU 5.25m. towards port facilities in Montego Bay, ECU 16m. towards a container terminal in Kingston and ECU 9m. for power transmission. It anticipated further lending of ECU 30m. during the period of EDF 8.

For the year 2000 the EU has provided direct budgetary support of ECU 34m., drawing from EDF 8, to sustain the government's economic reform programme.

Trinidad and Tobago

The second largest Commonwealth Caribbean country, Trinidad and Tobago has an economy almost equal in size to that of Jamaica ($6.1bn.) but a population half its size. The result is a GNP per capita at $4,750, twice that of Jamaica. Built upon a well established oil and gas industry, the economy has a relatively diversified economy, with downstream steel, ammonia and methanol production. Light manufacturing and tourism also contribute to the economy. The agricultural sector is dominated by the production of cane sugar and its by-product, rum. Rum is Trinidad and Tobago's principal export to the EU, accounting for 30 per cent of their ECU 377m. of exports in 1998, followed by Acyclic alcohols (22 per cent), petroleum (18 per cent) and sugar (5 per cent). The Sugar Protocol is estimated to have contributed an additional ECU 9.9m. above world prices in foreign exchange per annum to the country.

Through the 70s the economy had grown rapidly as it benefited from higher oil prices. However the fall in oil prices in the early 80s and reduced oil production, resulted in stagnation in the economy. Between 1979 and 1989 the economy failed to grow. In response, in 1989 the government adopted a structural reform package similar to that of Jamaica - devaluation, reduced public expenditure and reform of the tax system. In 1993 the government floated the Trinidadian dollar, with a consequent 30 per cent devaluation against the US dollar. The EU provided ECU 3m. SAS in 1994 to assist in the reform process.

The result has been a gradual reduction in the public sector deficit, from 4.5 per cent GNP in 1989 to only 0.4 per cent in 1999 and inflation has fallen from 11.4 per cent to 2.9 per cent. The balance of trade has generally maintained a $300m. surplus, although the current account was only just in surplus in 1999. The principle financial problem facing Trinidad is the size of the external debt, at $2,653m., with a debt/GDP ratio of 39 per cent and a debt service of $375m. in 1999. However it is estimated that 21 per cent of the population are now living in poverty.

Although the second largest recipient of EU aid allocation under EDFs 1 to 7, over the years 1990-97 Trinidad and Tobago has only received $86m. in disbursements. A number of projects have encountered unspecified problems, especially the ECU 17.5m. Solomon Hochoy Highway Rehabilitation Programme, which may account for this relatively low figure. EU assistance only really became important after the recession in the 1980s. A total of ECU 9.7m. was provided to support structural adjustment in 1993. EDF 7 also funded road rehabilitation (ECU 16m.), small farm development (ECU 5m.), small enterprise support (ECU 2m.) and rural electrification (ECU 2m.). A number of smaller projects have also been supported including water supply improvement, health worker training and school improvement. Assistance has also been provided to the Tourism Development Authority and the Export Development Corporation.

EDF 8 includes a NIP of ECU 21m. 50 per cent of this was allocated to economic diversification and employment creation and specifically to projects to encourage the development of small and medium sized firms, increasing the competitiveness of the non-oil sector, the growth of tourism, especially on Tobago, and the enhancement of the competitiveness of manufacturing and services. This priority complements the shift of government resources away from the energy sector and the general economic strategy outlined in their Medium Term Policy Framework. The second priority of EDF 8 aid is poverty alleviation, to which 35 per cent of NIP funds were allocated. Again this supports the governments strategy. In recent years a quarter of all public sector investment has been in social infrastructure. Trinidad and Tobago also received ECU 4.3m. SAS and the EIB allocated ECU 30m. for possible investment.

The Smaller Island Economies

Antigua and Barbuda

With the highest per capita income of the small island ACPs ($8990) Antigua and Barbuda are highly dependent upon tourism, accounting for 60 per cent of GDP. During the 1980s this sector, together with manufacturing and an inflow of investment (equivalent to 12.4 per cent GDP p.a.), sustained a growth rate of 7 per cent. The recession of the 1990s reduced the GDP growth rate to 3 per cent, but the economy soon recovered, growing 4.6 per cent in 1999. High levels of unemployment have been dealt with by expanding public sector employment. This, together with the abolition of income tax in 1976 and inefficient revenue collection, has led to a significant deterioration in public finances and accumulation of a mainly commercial foreign debt burden of $467m.; equal to 80 per cent of GDP. Trade with the EU has seen the deficit increase significantly in the last few years. In 1990 this deficit was only ECU 18m., but by 1998 it had grown to ECU 159m. In 1999 the government's budget deficit was 6.8 per cent of GDP and the current account deficit $98m.

The Caribbean Development Bank and other funders have ceased to lend to the government. Under the 1995-2000 National Indicative Plan (NIP), agreed with the EU, the government committed itself to remedying deficiencies in the tax system, the introduction of efficient management and expenditure controls, the privatisation of government holdings, a reduction in employment in the public sector with a wage freeze and the reduction of debt. Unfortunately the government has also made substantial cuts to its investment programme, with the result that the social infrastructure is deteriorating. The road network is of particular concern in that its condition may have adverse long term consequences for the tourist industry.

The government is committed to a diversification programme, but so far this has had achieved little. However a seed supply programme has been launched to encourage cotton production, with technical support, and traditional cattle rearing is regarded as having considerable potential.

Two further problems face the country. There is international concern that the islands are involved with the thriving drugs trade, both as a staging post in its transport and in the process of money laundering through its poorly regulated banking sector. There is also political tension between Antigua and its smaller neighbour Barbuda. Land ownership and the relatively underdeveloped state of the smaller island has led its population of 1,500 to consider independence. The Barbudan economy is dependent upon two exclusive resorts and an environmentally damaging sand extraction company, none of which have strong linkages to the local economy. Remittances from 5,000 overseas Barbudians make an important contribution to sustaining the economy.

Of the ECU 16.9m. of EU assistance (Table 2.5) 38 per cent has been allocated to infrastructure improvements, 28 per cent to education and training, 21 per cent to agriculture and 5 per cent to technical assistance. Lomé I and II funding concentrated upon water conservation, road rehabilitation and livestock husbandry. Lomé III allocated 80 per cent of it's funds to improvements in the road network, while EDF 7 concentrated upon training, with the development of a hotel training centre and construction of a secondary school. The NIP agreed under EDF 8 totals ECU 4.5m. with 90 per cent to be allocated to education and training. Structural Adjustment Support (SAS) will also be provided if the government achieves agreements with the World Bank/IMF. Unfortunately the government has failed to fully utilise its Lomé allocations.

Between 1990 and 1997 Antigua and Barbuda received $21m. of EU aid. In addition the EIB has also provided a soft loan for the installation of radar navigation at the local airport. Emergency aid was provided in 1982 after a severe drought and in 1989 after hurricane Hugo.

Dominica

Lying between the French DOMs of Martinique and Guadeloupe this volcanic island is heavily dependent upon the production of bananas. These represent 90 per cent of the value of total exports, with two-thirds destined for the EU, worth ECU 20m. in 1998. The EU's Banana Regime is thus of particular importance to this country. High prices and increased production supported high rates of growth in the 1980s, averaging 5.7 per cent (1979-89), but this has not been sustained in the 1990s, with growth falling to 1.9 per cent in the years 1989-99. Increasing competition in the banana market, together with the impact of hurricane Debby in 1994, underlined the vulnerability of this economy. Recurring current account deficits have been more than offset by remittances from Dominicans working overseas and by official aid flows. In 1999 the trade deficit was $22m. and the mainly concessionary accumulated debt $110m., resulting in a debt/GDP ratio of 42 per cent.

With changes in the EU Banana Regime required with the creation of the single market, the need for diversification in economic activity became urgent. Thus the EU has supported a number of agricultural projects, including the production and processing of patchouli, and the further development of the nascent tourist industry. Despite the islands substantial potential, tourism represented only 3 per cent of GDP in 1995. Between 1990-97 Dominica has received $120m. of assistance, with EDF 8 contributing ECU 14.8m. The NIP of EDF 8 excludes support for the banana industry but allocates 92 per cent of its ECU 6.5m. funds to the continued development of tourism. ECU 49m. of EU aid has been spent upon the reconstruction of 40 miles of road, with a further ECU 2.1m. allocated for a Northern Link road. The EIB has also provided loans for the establishment of a water bottling plant and government involvement in a hydroelectricity scheme (ECU 3.8m.).

Being dependent upon the export of bananas and coconuts Dominica has also benefited from ECU 22m. of Stabex payments in 1994 and 1995. These payments, together with funds from SSA (Special System of Assistance for Bananas), have been focused upon increasing the competitiveness of the banana industry and diversification. Finally Dominica has been one of the Caribbean's beneficiaries of SAS. Macro economic reforms were initiated by the government in 1986 and for the period 1993-93 the EU has contributed ECU 5m. to support this programme.

Grenada

Grenada, with Carriacou and Petite Martinique, has traditionally been a major exporter of bananas, cocoa and nutmeg (Table 2.6). Of these three products it is the banana industry that has experienced a significant decline in recent years, with exports suspended in 1997 because of their low quality. But Grenada, with Indonesia, is the world's main producer of nutmeg. The vulnerability of the islands' dependence upon commodity production is well illustrated by the slump in world nutmeg prices in 1993, after the collapse of a minimum price agreement with Indonesia. Its subsequent replacement by a voluntary agreement has restored some stability to the world market and prices have recovered. Similarly international prices for cocoa have fluctuated significantly and the islands' crop has been reduced by infestation with the pink mealy bug. This infestation has also led to a ban on other fruit and vegetable exports to regional markets. However unlike bananas it is felt that these industries have a long-term competitive future. A development strategy based upon the processing of these traditional products is being pursued. Thus the EU has partly funded the establishment of a nutmeg distillation plant.

Table 2.6 Grenada Primary Exports

		ECU Million	
	1992	**1994**	**1996**
Bananas	2.5	0.32	0.47
Cocoa	2.26	2.55	2.24
Nutmeg	1.99	3.9	3.6
Mace	0.52	0.58	0.67
Fish	1.68	2.68	2.74

Source: Grenada Annual Economic and Social Review.

As in other islands there is a desire to expand the tourist industry, and in particular, the numbers of stay-over visitors. Although the islands received 267,000 cruise visitors in 1996 these spent an average of only ECU 16. By contrast the number of stay-over visitors was 108,000, spending an average of ECU 436 per head, and worth in total more than ten times that of cruise visitors in their overall contribution to the economy. One important element in the tourism development strategy is to enhance the linkages with the agricultural and craft sectors, ensuring that their products meet the needs of this expanding industry. With good international links through the Cuban constructed international airport at Point Salines, the only infrastructure weaknesses are the state of the local road network and the water supply. Twenty per cent of EDF 8 funds were allocated to the further development of the tourist industry in the island.

Growth averaged 5.5 per cent p.a. between 1979 and 1989, but the recession of the early 1990s hit Grenada particularly hard, with a contraction of 0.4 per cent in 1992 and only 0.7 per cent growth in 1993. Unemployment peaked at 27 per cent in 1994 and remained at 17.5 per cent in 1996 (more than 50 per cent in the 15-19 age group). The limited recovery was sustained by improved market conditions for the export of nutmeg and cocoa and the growth of the tourist industry, with the opening of two new hotels. However the recession exacerbated the already difficult problem of the state of the public finances. In 1986 the government had abolished income tax, to be replaced by VAT. However this proved difficult to collect and was replaced by a more limited Consumption Tax. Tax evasion remains a serious problem. Although an income tax on very high earners has been introduced, indirect taxes still account for 60 per cent of government revenues. All three major primary products are marketed through State Boards, who subsidised farmers' prices in those years when international prices collapsed. Although Grenada had been able to cover its recurrent expenditure, it had relied on aid to provide for its capital investment. With the increasing reluctance of aid donors to support middle-income LDCs and an accumulated external debt which equalled 52 per cent of GNP by 1992, the need for fiscal reform became acute. Thus in 1992 a Structural Adjustment Plan was initiated, including fiscal reform and the reduction in the size of the public sector. Two of the major local banks and the electricity utility have been privatised, while the post office, airport, port and television company are to be reorganised on commercial lines. By 1999 the government's budget deficit had fallen to $8m. (2.5 per cent GDP) and growth had risen to 8.2 per cent.

Under Lomé I to III Grenada received ECU 29.5m. including ECU 6.7m. of EIB loans, while under EDF 7 it received ECU 11.6m. The EU has funded road repairs (including 25 miles of farm roads), the sub-division of a state-owned farm into private small-holdings, tourism promotion and the enhancement of a local water supply, especially in the more densely populated and drier south of the island. The crucial problems of water supply have been recognised for many years and, with bilateral assistance, a comprehensive assessment of the water supply was undertaken, strengthening of the National Water and Sewerage Authority begun and capital works commenced. The EU is supporting this programme and has allocated 80 per cent of the funds available under the NIP of EDF 8 (ECU 5.2m.) to continuation of the work. The EU has also financed school improvements in the capital St. George's and the construction of an Agricultural Training School. Since 1981 Grenada has also received ECU 10.2m. in Stabex payments and ECU 2m. as structural adjustment support under EDF 7.

St. Christopher (St. Kitts) and Nevis

St. Christopher (also known as St. Kitts) and Nevis are part of the Leeward group of islands. St. Christopher is the headquarters of the Eastern Caribbean Central Bank, the governing body for the Organisation of Eastern Caribbean States common currency area (the Eastern Caribbean Dollar).

Their economies were dominated by the production of sugar for many centuries, but since the 1980s a successful attempt has been made to diversify the economy. In the 1960s Nevis ended sugar production completely. Nonetheless sugar remains an important export from ST. Christopher, with a value of $15m. in 1997, and employing between 30 per cent and 45 per cent of the total labour force. The EU is the most important and lucrative market for the islands sugar exports, offering prices three times those of world levels under the EU's Sugar Regime. These exports were worth ECU 8m. in 1998, which represented 72 per cent of the value of the country's exports to the EU.

Tourism has been an important source of growth in recent years, with 165,000 visitors in 1996 contributing ECU 60.6m. to the economy. Serious attempts are also being made to establish an off-shore finance industry. Nevis has already achieved considerable success in becoming a base for off-shore company registrations. More than 10,000 companies are now registered in its jurisdiction, generating revenues of $2m. per annum.

Large scale manufacturing is not viable in such a small territory, nonetheless since the 1970s the government has consciously been attempting to attract light industry. St. Kitts now has a number of small scale production companies, including electronics, and has recently seen the establishment of IT and computer operations. The islands' education policy has focused upon providing the IT skills required by this sector. Manufactured exports were worth $24m. in 1997.

Overall the economy sustained 6.5 per cent per annum GDP growth between 1985 and 1988, although Hurricane Hugo and drought reduced growth to 3.6 per cent in the subsequent four years. Growth rates recovered and reached 7 per cent in 1997 before falling back to 1.1 per cent in 1998. Per capita incomes are relatively high at $6,420. The government maintains a budget deficit equal to 5.7 per cent GDP, a current account deficit of $78m. and outstanding debt is $136m., equal to 54 per cent of GNP.

Under Lomé I to III the islands received ECU 14.7m., including ECU 2.5m. in EIB loans to the St. Kitts and Nevis Development Bank for the funding of small and medium sized enterprises (SME). The EIB is also providing ECU 4m. of regional funding for a major extension to Nevis Airport to enhance tourist access to the island. Over half of EU aid has been directed at the social infrastructure, including a programme of construction of primary schools, improvements to the water and electricity supplies and the upgrading of the health sector. Under EDF 7 ECU 2m. had been allocated to the refurbishment of two major hospitals, while EDF 8 will provide ECU 3m. of further health service funding. This has supported a major effort by the government to reform and upgrade health service provision.

St. Lucia

The most densely populated of the four volcanic Windward Islands, St. Lucia is heavily dependent upon banana production and tourism; the service sector now accounts for 70 per cent of GDP. 60 per cent of St. Lucia's exports go to the EU, of which bananas represent 80 per cent by value (worth ECU 50m. in 1998). The EU also provides 25 per cent of St. Lucia's imports. Although over the years 1985-90 the economy grew at an average rate 8.7 per cent per annum, as both banana production and tourism expanded, this disguises considerable instability. In 1986 growth was 14.9 per cent, but in 1987 it fell to only 1.7 per cent before recovering to 12.7 per cent in 1988. The recent problems in the banana industry and the impact of hurricane Debby in 1994, underlined the vulnerability of the economy. The economy grew 3.1 per cent in 1999, but the current account remained in deficit at $54m. It has accumulated $184m. of outstanding foreign debt (30 per cent GDP).

Diversification of economic activity has been an important objective of the government for many years. In the agricultural sector diversification into the production of non-traditional crops such as breadfruit, peppers, mangoes and plantains, has been encouraged. The EU has supported this strategy in its ECU 39m. aid programme, with funding of livestock development and resettlement projects. The latter involved the redistribution of land and provision of road access in two valleys (Roseau and Mabouya). As well as encouraging the production of non-traditional crops it was also intended to address the problem of urban migration. The EU has also funded improvements to the major local market (Castries) to encourage the consumption of local produce.

The EU has supported the usual package of island projects,

including road construction, drainage and land conservation, tourism promotion studies and the provision of tertiary college facilities. EDF 7 assistance concentrated upon the social infrastructure, especially the development of the Victoria Hospital. Improvements in the island's health service will continue to be the priority for EDF 8 which will provide ECU 6m. The EIB has provided ECU 12.7m. to fund a study of geo-thermal energy, two loans for SMEs and for electricity supply development. St. Lucia has also been a major beneficiary of Stabex funds in compensation for instability in St. Lucia's banana earnings. Between 1992 and 1995 these payments totaled ECU 44.36m. These funds have been aimed at improving the competitiveness of the banana industry, economic diversification and general budgetary support.

St. Vincent and the Grenadines

St. Vincent is the largest island in the Grenadines chain. As with St. Lucia the islands are heavily dependent upon banana production and a growing tourism industry. Bananas represent half of all export earnings (41 per cent of exports to the EU) and benefit from the preferential access of the EU Banana Regime. Steady growth in the 1980s (5.9 per cent per annum 1979-89) has been compromised by changes in the banana market and a succession of hurricanes (especially Allen in 1980) and tropical storms. Between 1989 and 1999 the growth rate averaged only 3.3 per cent per annum and in 1996 it had fallen to only 1 per cent, with accompanying high levels of unemployment. By 1999 however the growth had recovered to 4 per cent. As is usual in these small islands the current account is in deficit, at $71m. External finance has been provided by grants and concessional loans resulting in a debt ratio of 49 per cent of GDP. Again the government's strategy has been one of general diversification and encouragement of non-traditional agricultural products.

Under Lomés I to III EU aid was directed at the health sector with the funding of several clinics and the development of Kingstown's hospital. Lomé III focused on a major rural resettlement project with the development of the Orange Hill Estate. This involves the creation of 400 diversified small farms with supporting infrastructure and agricultural services. A bottled water plant was also established on the estate. A similar project was funded at Mount Wyne-Peter's Hope under EDF 7. The development of Bequia airport has been the largest EDF funded project in the Eastern Caribbean. Opening in 1992 the airport received ECU 18.5m. of assistance. The EIB has provided ECU 6.9m. in loans to the national electricity company VINLEC and funding for SMEs in the industrial, agro-industrial and tourism sectors - with DEVCO, the development bank, and the Caribbean Financial Services Corporation. EDF 8 will provide ECU 6m., 85 per cent of which will be allocated to education, in particular the EU will support the development of a Community College. Substantial Stabex funds, of ECU 53.3m. over the period 1993-96, have again been used to enhance the international competitiveness of the banana industry and to assist with diversification.

British Dependencies (OCT)

The Overseas Countries and Territories of the members of the European Community have received special treatment since its inception. The Treaty of Rome provided for an 'association of Overseas Countries and Territories' with the object of promoting their development and establishing 'close economic relations between them and the Community as a whole' (Art. 131). It is in these provisions for the OCTs that the origins of all EU development policy lie. Thus in 1957 it was the Implementing Convention that established the first EDF for the OCTs and provided trade concessions. Since that time the EC Council has adopted Decisions at five yearly intervals, paralleling the renegotiations of the Lomé Conventions for the ACPs. The 1991 Decision (91/482/EEC) covered a ten year period like Lomé IV, with a mid-term revision (97/803/EC).

The OCTs are eligible for all the various forms of EDF and EIB assistance - Stabex, Sysmin, programmable aid, regional aid - however they also have a more advantageous trade regime with the EU than the ACP states. Since 1991 all products originating in the OCTs have unlimited tariff-free access to the EU, including CAP products. These concessions are non-reciprocal. However 'rules of origin' requirements remain. But besides products arising solely from the OCT itself, or where imported materials undergo 'sufficient processing', OCT preferences remain if inputs are imported from an ACP state (cumulation rule). However abuse of cumulation in the case of sugar and rice has led to restrictions for these two products since 1993. Free entry for OCT sugar exports is now limited to 3,000 tonnes and 160,000 tonnes for rice, with a possible additional 20,000 tonnes depending on market conditions. In specific cases the OCTs may also be given temporary exemption from the rules of origin requirements to encourage the establishment of new industries.

Under EDF 7 the twelve British OCTs were allocated ECU 15.5m. and under EDF 8 ECU 19.2m. of programmable aid (Table 2.7). All the Communities OCTs were allocated a total of ECU 200m. under EDF 8, including ECU 35m. of loans from the EIB and ECU 5.5m. for Stabex. The 1991 Decision had improved the financial arrangements by making all project funds grants, emphasised regional cooperation with other OCTs and ACPs and had introduced decentralised cooperation for local communities. Since 1992 the NIP has been agreed locally.

Table 2.7 Aid Allocation to the Overseas Territories

	ECU Million			
	NIP	**EIB**	**EDF 8**	**EDF 4-7**
Anguilla	3	0	3	7.8
British Virgin Islands	2.5	2	4.5	1.6
Cayman Islands	0	2	2.5	14.9
Montserrat	4	0	4	11.4
Turks & Caicos Islands	4	0	4	7.9
Netherlands Antilles	23.8	7	30.8	
(& Aruba)	(7.9)	(2)	(10.4)	183.2

Source: EU Social/Regional Funds 1994-99.

The United Kingdom has five dependencies in the Caribbean region. Of the five territories the Cayman islands are the largest, with a population of 26,000, the smallest Anguilla with 9,000 (see Table 2.2). Since the eruption of Montserrat's volcano in 1998 the future of the island's 11,000 population is in doubt.

The four remaining island groups share similar economic structures, with important financial sectors and 'up market' tourism. In Anguilla tourism accounts for 30 per cent of GDP with rapidly expanding vegetable production to meet the demands of the industry. Skill shortages are presenting problems and unemployment is low. The EU has funded a number of infrastructure projects including a new electricity station, water supply and road improvements. The EIB has also loaned funds for a hotel development.

The fifty small British Virgin Islands were particularly badly affected by Hurricane Hugo in 1989 but rapidly recovered. Growth was 8.5 per cent in 1990 and a rate of 3-5 per cent was expected over the years 1993-96. Tourism accounts for 25 per cent of GDP and the territory is host to a growing off-shore financial sector. Again EU assistance has been concentrated on enhancing the local water and power supplies and port developments. Funding has also been provided to the local community college.

Although the three Cayman islands are also dependent upon tourism and financial services both sectors have experienced a slowdown in growth in recent years. Air access has been identified as one of the limiting factors on the expansion of the tourist industry and as a result the EU has contributed ECU 1m. to the upgrading of the Cayman Brac airport. Funds have also been provided towards a new Community College, reflecting the EU's emphasise upon human capital investment, and EIB loans towards upgrading electricity and water supplies on Grand Cayman. The high per capita income ($18,520) has excluded the islands from receipt of grants under EDF 7.

Finally, by contrast, the eight inhabited Turks and Caicos islands have experienced strong rates of growth in both their tourist and financial sectors in recent years. Again transport infrastructure has been identified as a limiting factor in the further expansion of the tourist industry and it is to meet this need that the EU has funded a new jetty on South Turk, an air terminal on South Caicos and further transport studies. EDF 7 funds (ECU 3.7m.) have been allocated to enhancing the water and sewage systems of the main tourist island Providenciales, which increasingly has attracted the local population for employment.

Conclusion

As can been seen in this brief review of the recent economic history of these small, predominantly island economies, they share many common characteristics which are responsible for their vulnerability to external shocks. Their agricultural sectors are exposed to the intermittent destruction of hurricanes and threatened by the vagaries of unstable world markets for their primary products. It was to reduce this exposure that special commodity regimes were established by colonial powers, creating protected metropolitan markets. The EU has continued this form of development assistance, particularly in regard to sugar and bananas, but these regimes are under threat from the requirements of the new World Trade Organisation.

Diversification is regarded as the core of any island development strategy and tourism is usually seen as offering the greatest potential. The EU has focused upon tourism-related transport infrastructure, marketing and training in many of its aid programmes. Certainly during the 1960s it was responsible for much of the growth in the island economies of the Caribbean. Unfortunately the world recessions of the 1970s and 80s illustrated how unstable demand could be in this competitive economic sector. The increasing popularity of cruising is also reducing the benefits of the industry to many island economies. The development of tourism is also associated with a substantial increase in import dependence, both during construction and for non-indigenous food imports, and the environmental impact can be significant. Nonetheless by 1997 tourism earnings represented 76 per cent of total exports for St. Lucia, 61 per cent for Antigua, 55 per cent for Barbados, 44 per cent for St. Vincent and 28 per cent for Belize.

An alternative strategy adopted by some islands, especially the British Overseas Territories, has been the development of off-shore finance. However increasing concern has been expressed by both the US and EU over the level of regulation and their use for money 'laundering' and tax evasion. It is by no means certain that the international financial environment will remain as accommodating of these 'off shore' centres as it has in the past.

However the high levels of education in many of the Caribbean islands may offer considerable potential for the development of IT industries. Data processing or software development are not constrained by the traditional problems of high cost transport links and small local markets.

With their high dependence upon imports, deterioration in the international terms of trade, or decline in their export earnings, has a major impact upon their economies. Most islands sustain a persistent balance of payments deficit. As a result of these problems many of these states have accumulated substantial foreign debt. The extreme case is Guyana, with a debt: GDP ratio of 230 per cent. However Antigua (56 per cent), Jamaica (56 per cent), Grenada (54 per cent), St. Vincent (53 per cent), Dominica (42 per cent) and St. Kitts (40 per cent) all have significant liabilities. Aid flows are therefore important in financing these borrowings and providing balance of payments relief.

Although their small size offers the advantage that any aid commitments are relatively small in absolute terms, it also reduces their influence and importance in the corridors of power. The difficulties of such small states are graphically illustrated by the problems presented in defending their interests before the World Trade Organisation in the face of the US challenge to the EU's banana regime. To assist the ACP's negotiations in the WTO the EU is funding an advisory office in Geneva. But under the Cotonou Agreement there is considerable pressure to move towards separate regional agreements. This is being vociferously resisted by the Caribbean governments, who can see themselves being marginalised in future EU development policy. Indeed their relatively high per capita incomes are at the core of the difficulty of maintaining Lomé trade preferences that are compatible with the EU's WTO obligations, which only allows non-reciprocal trade concessions for the very low-income less developed countries.

The EU's aid programme in the region will have to continue to take account of the implementation problems which have been identified throughout the region (Ishmael, 1998). The small size of most of these states has produced difficulties in project preparation, implementation and appraisal. Most islands do not engage in an integrated approach to project and programme planning, and systems of internal communication are often weak. Development is often project driven, incrementalist and explicitly sectoral, rather than part of a coherent overall development strategy. There is also often a failure to appreciate the recurrent costs of projects that are initiated by donors but only funded for the short-run. At the regional level there are still inadequate mechanisms for sharing information and experience. International donors meanwhile continue to fail to coordinate their efforts and impose unreasonable demands upon local administrations. The EU's approach of NIP should foster an integrated approach to development policy and local 'ownership'. The need for capacity building in local administrations has also been clearly identified. The current reviews of EU aid administration should address some of the problems of administrative complexity and delayed disbursement of funds, while offering the opportunity for a greater degree of delegation to local representatives. Despite the possibly of choppy waters ahead these countries have high levels of literacy and good educational systems, and have exhibited a remarkable degree of political stability compared with many other developing countries. But their small size will always present unique political and economic problems to which attention will need to be paid.

References

Commonwealth Secretariat (1997), *A Future for Small States: Overcoming Vulnerability*, London.

Commonwealth Secretariat (1999), *Small States: Meeting Challenges in the Global Economy*, London.

Ishmael L. (1998), Small Island Developing States Programme of Action for Sustainable Development - Opportunities and Constraints: Seminar Paper, Small Island Developing States, Their Vulnerability, Programme for Action for Sustainable Development and Their Opportunities Post Lomé, Brussels.

3 The EU Banana Protocol

STEPHEN DEARDEN

The UK's preferential banana import regime was of considerable economic significance for a number of Commonwealth Caribbean island economies. However the move to a single EU market required the replacement of this regime with an EU wide scheme. This change was to prove problematic both for the Caribbean suppliers and for the EU. As we will see in the next chapter bananas were to become a focus of conflict not only between the ACPs and the EU, but also between EU member states and finally, and most significantly, with the USA. The EU Banana regime was to throw a critical light on the operations of the new WTO and to set the tone for the reform of the whole ACP preferential trading regime under Lomé, but the outcome is also of profound significance for a small number of developing countries within the ACP group, most of which are part of the Commonwealth Caribbean.

While Chapter 4 will review the political forces at work which were to determine the final outcome, this chapter will be considering the economic context and consequences of this reform. Beginning with a review of the EU's banana import trends and the significance of banana production to the islands of the Caribbean, it then reviews the options for reform. It outlines the reforms themselves and their immediate impact upon the EU banana market. Finally it reviews the challenges to the EU's trade preferences under the WTO and the subsequent changes to the regime.

The European Banana Market Pre-1993

The EU accounts for approximately one-third of world imports of bananas, which in 1992 were worth ECU 20bn. Prior to 1993 the EU banana market had been fragmented by national import controls. Half of the EU's member states operated such schemes covering 40 per cent of EU imports and ensuring preference for their traditional colonial suppliers and overseas territories (DOMs - Departements d'Outre-Mer). Spain obtained most of its

Table 3.1 Banana Imports 1992

'000 Tonnes (% Total Imports)

	D	E	F	I	ND	P	UK
Canary Isles		345 (100)					
Cape Verde						2(2)	4(1)
Ivory Coast			130(24)	6(1)			7(1)
Cameroon			79(15)	24(5)			
Belize							28(5)
Honduras	102(7)			25(5)		21(2)	15(3)
Nicaragua	17(1)				2(1)	2(2)	
Costa Rica	253(18)			63(13)	6(3)	14(14)	37(7)
Panama	280(20)			67(14)		6(6)	
Guadeloupe			115(21)				
Dominica				7(1)			45(8)
Martinique			197(37)				
Jamaica							75(14)
St. Lucia				11(2)			111(20)
St. Vincent				15(3)			56(10)
Grenada							6(1)
Columbia	271(20)			55(11)	14(7)	26(27)	21(4)
Suriname							30(6)
Ecuador	434(31)			100(21)	17(8)	22(23)	10(2)
Total	1,378	346	532	476	201	97	545

EU Total Imports – 4,038,988 tonnes.
Source: Eurostat.

bananas from the Canary Islands; Portugal from Madeira; France from Martinique and Guadeloupe, the Cameroons and the Ivory Coast; the UK from the Windward Islands, Belize (British Honduras) and Jamaica (Table 3.1).

In all the other Member States, except Germany, ACP imports entered duty-free under the Lomé Conventions, while the competing 'dollar' banana producers of Central and South America faced a Common External Tariff of 20 per cent. In Germany, the largest EU market for bananas, all imports were tariff-free and the market was exclusively supplied by the more efficient dollar producers, who with their large scale, irrigated, plantation-based production obtain yields double those of the ACP producers. Cost comparisons are difficult, but whereas Ecuador can produce bananas at $162 per tonne and Costa Rica at $179 per tonne (f.o.b. variable costs), the Windward Islands were averaging $485 per tonne and Jamaica $391 per tonne (f.o.b. total costs) in 1992-3 (FAO and CIRAD).

Table 3.2 Banana Imports 1992

ECU '000

	D	E	F	I	ND	P	UK
Canary Isles		297258					
Cape Verde						1175	
Ivory Coast			83956	2552			2167
Cameroon			52172	9741			5127
Belize							15604
Honduras	44057			10993		4068	5340
Nicaragua	7707				521	525	
Costa Rica	111251			27975	2308	2388	15770
Panama	124743		28218			413	
Guadeloupe			65424				
Dominica				3001			28926
Martinique			111634				
Jamaica							46626
St. Lucia				4511			70810
St.Vincent				6023			35746
Grenada							3850
Columbia	116539			23114	3904	4960	8829
Suriname							15288
Ecuador	190741			43016	5694	5544	4228
Total	603793	297264	321756	220538	83779	19505	321624

Total Imports - ECU 2041793.
Source: Eurostat.

The removal of the internal barriers to trade with the creation of the EU's single market required the elimination of these different national import controls and raised the spectre of the domination of the EU market by the dollar producers.

Import Trends

In 1982 the EC10 imported 1.87 million metric tonnes (mt.) of bananas (7kg. per capita), approximately one-third of world imports. Of this total 17.6 per cent (0.33mt.) were imported from the ACP countries. Over the ten years to 1992 EC12 imports doubled to 4.0mt. (10.5kg. per capita), as did ACP exports to 0.7m. tonnes, worth ECU 413m. However imports declined in later years, falling to 3.46mt. in 1995 (9.6 kg. per capita). Over this period the ACP share of EU imports has been unstable, peaking at 25 per cent in 1986, a share it returned to in the 1990s. The increase ıı total imports and decline in the ACP market share in 1991 and 1992 has been explained by many commentators (Read 1994) as evidence of the attempt by Multi National Company (MNC) dollar banana importers to increase their market share in anticipation of the new banana import regime. Since the late 1980s Latin American production had been rapidly expanding at a rate well in excess of the increase in world demand.

As can be seen from Table 3.1 Germany represented one-third of the EU market for bananas, supplied exclusively by low priced dollar banana producers. Germany has maintained the highest per capita banana consumption in the Community. In the period 1980 to 1985 it averaged 8.5kg. per capita and experienced the largest increase in later years, peaking at 16.9kg. per capita in 1992. Spain, Italy, France and the UK each account for 10 per cent to 14 per cent of the total market. Of these other larger markets the UK has experienced by far the highest rate of growth of consumption - from an average of 5.7kg. per capita over the years 1980-1985 consumption rose 84 per cent to 10.5kg. per capita by 1995. The UK imported 90 per cent of its bananas from ACP countries, with 52 per cent coming from the Windward Islands. France imported 59 per cent of its bananas from the Overseas Territories of Guadeloupe and Martinique, while Spain imported all of its bananas from the Canary Islands. Except for its imports from Somalia (15 per cent) Italy relied on dollar banana imports.

The distribution of bananas was dominated by three US MNCs - Chiquita (formally the United Fruit Company), Dole (formally Castle and Cook and acquirer of Standard Fruit) and the Del Monte Corporation. The latter entered the industry in 1967 through the purchase of the West Indies Fruit Company. These companies were principally concerned with supplying the US market from Central and South America, but through subsidiaries (e.g. United Fruit's Elders) they also supplied Europe. Approximately 64 per cent of world exports of bananas were controlled by these MNCs and in 1991 Chiquita supplied 25 per cent of EU imports, Dole 11 per cent and Del Monte 8 per cent (Arthur D. Little 1995). Their vertical integration had allowed them to resist new entrants. Nonetheless, in recent years they have withdrawn from the direct ownership of their specialist shipping and reduced their own plantation production. In 1974-1976 United Fruit produced 75 per cent of its bananas from its own plantations, but Standard Fruit relied on contracting independent producers for 53 per cent of its bananas and Del Monte for 57 per cent.

The Commonwealth Caribbean Producers

Banana exports are important to a number of Commonwealth countries in the Caribbean, all of whom have preferential access to the EU under the Lomé Convention.

Bananas are of least importance to Belize and Jamaica in the Commonwealth Caribbean. For Belize banana exports in 1992 represented only 15 per cent of the value of its total exports earnings of ECU 104.7m. However the volume of exports to the UK, its only EU market, subsequently doubled from 26,580 tonnes in 1989 to 54,109 tonnes in 1996 and now represent 25 per cent of its total export earnings. The banana industry is particularly important to the south of the country and provides the transport infrastructure, especially the only weekly shipping link.

Banana production in Jamaica began in the 19th century, initially with exports to the USA. Elders and Fyffes (taken over by the United Fruit Company of the USA in 1913) dominated the UK-Caribbean trade until the 1950s, with exports peaking at 300,000 tonnes. The collapse of production in the early 1950s as a result of disease and hurricane damage, was followed by replanting and an increase in production . This led to a 'banana war' between Fyffes, supplying Jamaican bananas to the UK, and Geest supplying bananas from the Windward Islands. In 1996 the two companies agreed to split the UK market 52 per cent: 48 per cent and not to import non-Caribbean bananas except in cases of inadequate supply. The selection of Jamaican bananas lay with the statutory Jamaican Banana Board (formed in 1947) which, subject to political pressure, failed to maintain quality controls (Nurse and Sandiford 1995 p. 25). By the 1970s the industry was in decline, in 1974 it exported only 66,800 tonnes. In 1981 a fundamental review of the industry took place, with the privatisation of the banana estates and the formation of BECO (the Banana Export Company), controlled by the growers, to help in restructuring production and marketing. Investment, funded by the Commonwealth Development Corporation (£11.8m.) and the International Finance Corporation (£3.8m.) has been concentrated in three large plantations and yields, as a consequence, are comparable to those of the Latin and Central American suppliers. By 1990 it produced 128,000 tonnes of bananas and exported 63,181 tonnes to the UK (Table 3.1), its only EU market. As the volume of bananas exported to the EU has increased they have taken an increasing share of Jamaica's total banana exports. In 1989 Jamaica exported 43,000 tonnes, but only 20,000 tonnes to the Community. By 1991 93 per cent of its banana exports were to the EU, totaling 70,000 tonnes, and by 1996 these had increased even further to 90,000 tonnes. However these subsequently fell back to 62,000 tonnes by 1998. But Jamaica is a diversified economy and banana exports represented only 4 per cent of its $1157m. of merchandised exports, although 34 per cent of its $132m. of non-fuel primary exports. Nonetheless with a national unemployment rate of 22.4 per cent in 1993, the 30,000 jobs in Jamaica's banana industry were an important source of employment; 3.3 per cent of total employment and 12.3 per cent of all agricultural employment.

The Windward Islands

The Windward Islands of Dominica, Grenada, St. Lucia, St. Vincent and the Grenadines are all independent countries with a total population of 434,000. Although small economies they have been relatively successful, with an average growth rate of 4.0 per cent to 4.5 per cent over the period 1985 to 1994 and a GNP per capita of $2,675 in 1994. Unlike Jamaica bananas are of far greater significance to their economies with 30 per cent of the cultivated area used for this crop. Bananas are one of the most labour intensive crops produced and account for between 33 per cent (Dominica and St. Lucia) and 70 per cent (St. Vincent) of all employment (Nurse and Sandiford 1995). The World Bank estimates that between 27,000 and 30,000 farmers produce bananas in the Islands.

Banana production for export had expanded rapidly in the 1950s, encouraged by the UK government as a substitute for the declining sugar industry and as a challenge to Fyffes dominance of the UK market with their Jamaican bananas. First the large sugar estates diversified, to be followed by the smaller farmers. Production peaked in 1969 before the increase in costs following the 1972 oil price shock. Production was also adversely affected by hurricanes in 1979 and 1980. Estate production declined throughout the 1970s so that today bananas are principally produced by small and medium sized farmers. The average farm size in the Windward Islands is just under two acres (Gill and Gonazales 1995). It is estimated that banana production employed, directly and indirectly, 31 per cent of the Windward Islands labour force (House of Commons, Agricultural Committee 1992). Each island has a Producers' Association which has a statutory monopoly on the sale of bananas. These Associations in turn had an exclusive marketing contracts with Geest, which controlled 45 per cent of the UK market.

St. Lucia and St. Vincent only export to the EU and shared a substantial increase in their exports, increasing by 200 per cent and 170 per cent respectively, between 1982 and 1992. Banana exports for St. Lucia in

1993 at $51.1m. represented 41 per cent of all export earnings, while for St. Vincent they were 33 per cent of merchandised exports at $23m. Except for 1986 St. Lucia's share of the EU market had been steady at 3 per cent. However St. Vincent's exports have almost halved from their peak of 81,500 tonnes in 1990 to only 44,000 tonnes in 1996.

Dominica has shared in the increase in its volume of exports to the EU, doubling from 26,438 tonnes in 1982 to 55,932 tonnes in 1992, with their share of the EU market averaging 2 per cent. As with the other Windward Islands most of their exports went to the UK. By 1993 the value of these exports was $24m., 41 per cent of export earnings. Production absorbs 43 per cent of the agricultural labour force. However in the next three years exports declined. In 1996 they totalled only 39,000 tonnes.

Unlike the other Windward Islands, for Grenada the volume of banana exports are quite small and had fallen dramatically from 9,300 tonnes in 1982 to only 2,000 tonnes in 1996. Banana exports to the EU, its only market, earned $2.1m. in 1993, 7 per cent of merchandised exports. Cocoa and nutmeg are more import export crops than bananas, and banana production only involves 7 per cent of the agricultural labour force.

The real wholesale price obtained in the UK rose by approximately 50 per cent over the period 1966 to 1986 (Thomas 1989a), although in part this was affected by a change to the supply of higher cost higher quality produce. These trends contrast with a more volatile world free market price. Most of the fluctuation in Windward Island earnings from banana exports arises from variations in the volume of exports and fluctuations in the value of sterling against the US dollar, in which currency bananas are priced.

Although bananas are of considerable significance to all of the Windward Island economies the industry has developed few forward or backward linkages. Inputs are imported and little processing is required before export. Farmers' earnings from banana production have not been channelled into alternative crops nor into tradeable manufactures. Dependence on banana production therefore remains high, except in Grenada. Although the Island governments have been attempting to improve their competitiveness with dollar bananas by increasing yields and reducing post-harvest losses, they have also been encouraging diversification of their agricultural sectors.

In Dominica potato production has been encouraged to substitute for imports and in St. Lucia locally grown fresh vegetables to supply the tourist industry. To replace bananas as the dominant export crop Dominica and St. Lucia have promoted the production of mangos, grapefruits, avocados and oranges, while a number of countries have attempted to export cut flowers. However the small plots and poor basic infrastructure make the competitive production of alternative crops difficult. In the case of Jamaica for example, exports of winter vegetables to the US have faced non-tariff barriers, while melon and tomato production proved too expensive. A recent report by the FAO (1996) surveyed the experience of a number of attempts at diversification away from banana production, including the TROPRO project in the West Indies in the late 1980s. The latter had shown some success in encouraging the export of mangoes and avocados but was constrained by 'the slow pace of infrastructure development'. It is therefore not surprising that these projects have met with only limited success and over the last thirty years the importance of secondary crops has actually declined.

Bananas remain a far more attractive crop, with their labour-intensive capital-saving production, quick returns and fast recovery from hurricane damage. They are also intimately linked with food self-sufficiency since the provision of fertilisers, through the Banana Growers Associations, is important to inter-planted root crops. Indeed it is suggested some farmers grow small quantities of bananas solely to obtain access to fertilisers on credit (Gill and Gonzales 1995). Unlike the newly promoted crops, bananas are efficiently marketed through the Producers Associations and Fyffes. Furthermore the high banana prices of some recent years have undermined any attempt to encourage farmers to diversify (Thomas 1989b).

The Policy Options

Under the fragmented pre-1993 EU regime the CET (Common External Tariff) of 20 per cent on banana imports only applied to certain states. Germany imported bananas duty-free while the UK offered duty-free access to ACP producers, with dollar banana imports controlled by import licensing. These dollar banana import licenses guaranteed access to the UK for a minimum of 30,000 tons annually, with additional licenses should traditional suppliers fail to meet domestic demand. Similarly 60 per cent of the French market was supplied by its Overseas Departments of Martinique and Guadeloupe, with further imports supplied by African Franc zone countries such as Cameroon. Dollar imports were subject to licensing which would only be granted if prices exceeded certain levels. Italy granted free access to ACP imports, with Somalia being offered preferential status, but restricted other imports to a global quota which in 1983 was 270,000 tons. Spain was supplied by the Canary Islands and Portugal by Madeira and both excluded supplies from other sources.

The overall effect of these existing trade policies had been to reduce world prices, subsidise favoured supplying countries and consumers in Germany, at the expense of dollar producers and of consumers in the remaining EU member states who restricted access to their markets. The estimated welfare loss to EU consumers of this system of import controls ranged from $642m. (Read 1994) to $1.6bn. (Borrell and Yang 1992; McInerney and Peston 1992) and the net cost to the EU between $527m. (Read 1994) and $575m. (Borrell and Yang 1992).

Faced with the demands of establishing a single market a number of options presented themselves to the Community. The problem could have been circumvented by allowing derogations to some of the Member States to continue their import controls. Although the perishable nature of the product and the dominance of the market by a limited number of importing companies might have made this possible, it offered no long-term solution. At the other extreme a free market could have been established following the German example.

The consequences for EU consumers, ACP suppliers and dollar producers of the various policy options have been examined in a number of studies.

Borrell and Yang (1990) evaluated the impact of four policy options; the extension of free trade to the whole Community, the adoption of a CET of 20 per cent on all imports, a system of deficiency payments and direct aid payments. The adoption of free trade in bananas was found to raise EU consumption by 9 per cent. Dollar banana imports would have increased by 12 per cent but ACP suppliers would have seen their exports fall by 46 per cent. Although EU consumers experienced a gain in economic welfare of $386m. annually and dollar exporters gained $61m. from access to the EU market and higher world prices, ACP countries lost $209m. each year. These loses were substantial when compared to the value of ACP banana exports to the EU which totalled $576m. in 1987.

Turning to the extension of a CET of 20 per cent to Germany, with continuing ACP duty-free access to the Community, German consumers experienced a substantial welfare loss of $85m. Alternatively the ACP tariff concessions could be abandoned. This produced a smaller global welfare loss than the previous case since a non-discriminatory tariff allows rationalisation of production between exporters. However such rationalisation was again be at the expense of the ACP producers who experienced substantial loses. To address this problem a deficiency payment system could have been established financed by a CET. Such deficiency payments would be received by the ACPs to cover the difference between the world price they would receive and their current protected prices. Borrell and Yang calculate that a tariff of 16.7 per cent would be required to finance such a scheme. Again German consumers would have been the major losers of such an approach.

However Borrell and Young favoured direct aid payments financed by a CET of 16.1 per cent. Deficiency payments would encourage production by the ACP exporters through artificially raising prices. By contrast direct aid minimises the distortion to world trade and allows the targeting of assistance to diversification of the ACP economies. They estimate that direct aid payments to ACP exporters would total $273m. annually, an increase of $64m. on the existing level of implicit benefit from discriminatory tariffs. However it would still result in the same 47 per cent reduction in ACP banana exports as in the free trade scenario.

Davenport and Page (1991) carried out a similar simulation of the alternative regimes that might be introduced. They examined three cases; removal of quantitative limits on imports with a CET, deficiency payments and a quota system. With only a CET restricting imports, without any ACP preference, prices would have fallen to those prevailing in the member states with unrestricted dollar banana imports – i.e. Belgium, Denmark, Ireland and the Netherlands. This was approximately ECU 4.5 per kilo, compared with a price of ECU 7 for EC bananas, ECU 4.5 - 6 for African imports and ECU 6 for Windward Island bananas. The competitiveness of ACP bananas is such that their market share falls from 52 per cent to 28 per cent, reducing their export earnings by 75 per cent. Were the ACPs to be compensated for these losses at a rate of ECU 165 per tonne Davenport and Page estimate that the cost to the EU would total ECU 200m. (based upon 1988 prices and volumes).

Deficiency payments, to supplement EU and ACP producers incomes from world prices in a free market, would still encourage these producers to become more efficient. However unless the deficiency payments differentiated between producing countries the least competitive (e.g. the Windward Islands) would still have lost market share. The cost of such a scheme could have been high unless financed, as suggested by Borrell and Yang, from retaining a CET on dollar banana imports. Davenport and Page found that price guarantees at ECU 7 per kilo for EU producers and at ECU 5 per kilo for ACP suppliers, financed in part by a CET of 14 per cent, would still result in a 16 per cent fall in ACP exports and a decline in export earnings of 24 per cent.

A quota system would have involved establishing limits on EU imports of dollar bananas, with a lower CET. ACP bananas would have continued their unrestricted duty-free entry into the EU market. The larger the initial size of the dollar banana quota and the greater its growth rate, the lower would be the Community's price of bananas but the smaller the ACPs share of the market. The price of bananas would also be lower if an overall dollar import quota was established within which producers had to compete, perhaps by auction, for licenses.

It was also possible to adopt a mixed scheme, e.g. of deficiency payments and quotas. However any import regime would still have to reconcile the trade-off between the maintenance of ACPs market shares and the loss of EU consumer surplus from higher EU banana prices above the free-market world level.

The Reform of the EU Banana Regime

The Fourth Lomé Convention had committed the EU to ensuring that 'no ACP state shall be placed as regards access to its traditional markets and its advantages on those markets in a less favourable position than in the past or at present'. However in the negotiations of the Uruguay Round of the GATT the EU committed itself to the 'fullest possible liberalisation of trade in tropical products'. As these difficult negotiations continued they inevitably began to interact with the discussions taking place to establish a new Banana regime for the single European market. The threat existed of a challenge by the Latin American countries, under GATT procedures, to any adoption of a quota system. Indeed the EU was already constrained by the existing GATT rules not to raise the average tariff on bananas. Thus the elimination of the German tariff-free quota on dollar bananas would require an offsetting reduction in any CET from 20 per cent to 14 per cent.

The Commission's response to the need for a Banana Protocol was not issued until August 1992 (COM 359/92). The new scheme was to be a combination of deficiency payments and import quotas. For the EU's own producers (Guadeloupe, Martinique, Canaries, Madeira and Crete) deficiency payments would be limited to 854,000 tonnes (cf. imports of 645,000 tonnes in 1990); ECU 1,000 per hectare would also be offered as compensation to any farmer who ceased production. ACP imports from the eleven traditional suppliers would continue to enter duty-free up to their 1990 level; but any greater volume of 'non-traditional' ACP imports and all dollar bananas, would be subject to a basic quota of 2m. tonnes. This would be increased if projected demand and supply conditions in the EU market suggested that a shortage might emerge. The proposal also introduced the 'partnership principle' whereby 30 per cent of import licenses would be reserved for importers who have partnership agreements with Community or ACP suppliers. As import licenses generate monopoly rents for importers, the Commission anticipated cross-subsidisation, with the profits acquired from the import of quota dollar bananas covering the additional costs of importing EU and ACP fruit. It would also have provided some protection to ACP suppliers from predatory activities by 'dollar' importers. However in the face of strong opposition from Germany and the Benelux countries and with the GATT negotiations seeking to remove non-tariff barriers to trade, the import quota proposal had to be abandoned.

The final version of the new banana regime (CEC 404/93) introduced a tariff-quota but preserved duty-free access for ACP imports up to their traditional level. Traditional imports were initially limited to 622,000 tonnes, but the final figure is much more generous at 1.7m. tonnes. This is now defined as the best ever import figure for each ACP state before 1991 and allows for existing expansion plans where appropriate (ie. Belize 55,000 tonnes: Jamaica, 105,000 tonnes; St. Lucia 127,000 tonnes; St. Vincent 82,000 tonnes; Grenada 14,000 tonnes; Dominica 71,000 tonnes). This method of calculating the import limit would only constrain Jamaica in the short-run, but given the rising export trend for Belize, St. Lucia, St. Vincent and Dominica, it would represent a serious constraint in the long term unless the EU conceded an upward revision.

For dollar banana imports and ACP imports in excess of their traditional level the EU adopted a tariff-quota of 2m. tonnes, subsequently revised to 2.5m. tonnes with the enlargement of the Community. Within this limit imported dollar bananas will pay a duty of ECU 100 per tonne, and 'non-traditional' ACP bananas will continue to enter duty-free. Imports greater than 2.5 m. tonnes will be subject to a tariff of ECU 850 per tonne (a rate of 170 per cent) on dollar bananas and ECU 750 per tonne on non-traditional ACP bananas. The overall quotas of 3.71m. tonnes compare with imports of 3.4m. tonnes in 1992.

Even with a ECU 100 per tonne tariff advantage it would be unlikely that importers would substitute non-traditional ACP bananas for dollar fruit as part of their 2.0m. tonne quota. Therefore to guarantee their market share the 'partnership principle' was formally abandoned but replaced by the simple reservation of 30 per cent of the licences (category 'B' licences) within the 2m. tonne import quota for importers of 'traditional' ACP and EU bananas. This provided an incentive to ensure access to the EU market for ACP fruit, in order for the importer to continue to retain their valuable licence to import the more profitable dollar bananas. Nonetheless there remained a concern either that the profit margins likely to be made on quota dollar bananas would be insufficient to cover the additional costs of

ACP fruit, or that they may be excessive, allowing the cross subsidisation of non-quota dollar fruit and the capture of additional market share. The remaining elements of the Regulation, which came into force on the 1st July 1993, followed the original proposal.

The Special System of Assistance

At the same time as introducing a Banana Regime to control imports into the Community, the Commission had proposed additional assistance for those ACP countries that were likely to be adversely affected by the new regime (COM 465/92). Lomé IV had anticipated the problems for banana producers with the advent of the single market by offering financial assistance for diversification from its substantially increased ECU 1500m. Stabex fund. This offers grants to compensate for destabilising reductions in export earnings from the sale of any of 49 products. For the island economies products were eligible if they formed more than 1 per cent of a States export earnings, which was the case with bananas.

However the Commission wished to go further in assisting the ACP countries to adjust to the new market conditions after 1993. They therefore proposed that financial assistance was made available to those ACP states that prepared programmes to improve the quality, marketing and competitiveness of their bananas (Council Regulations 2686/94 and 2320/96). This Special System of Assistance (SSA) totalled ECU 95m., with ECU 78 allocated to seven traditional ACP banana exporting countries (ECU 17m. remaining unassigned) over three years. This should be contrasted with the ECU 185m. of support for EU producers over the same period. It was divided between income support - provided as compensation for reductions in banana export revenues, as with Stabex - and technical assistance. The latter dispersed the unutilised balance of the SSA and was assigned on a first-come first-served basis for individual projects. Belize subsequently received ECU 3.27m. as technical assistance, funding port and farm infrastructure and village improvements. Jamaica received ECU 7.8m. in income support and ECU 3.0m. in technical assistance. Aid was organised through a Banana Support Programme concentrating upon water management, disease control, input supplies and general extension work. For the Windward Islands the ECU 1.7m. of income support was used to finance recovery after the 1994 and 1995 hurricanes and the ECU 7.7m. of technical assistance to reform the organisation of the banana industry. It was intended that this additional funding should be temporary and continue only until stability returned to the banana market.

The relative inadequacy of this compensation becomes apparent when we consider the existing value to these countries of the original banana regime and contrast it with the value of their concessions under the new arrangements. If we regard the import prices (c.i.f. plus tariff) in the German market as an approximation of the 'free-trade' price in the early 1990s and compare this with the price obtained in the UK by the ACP exporters, the values indicated in Table 3.3 are derived. These figures must be treated with some care, especially as there is some evidence that the US MNC exporters were dumping bananas on the German market during these years. Under the new regime ACP fruit enters duty-free while dollar bananas face a duty of ECU 75 per tonne. The value of this concession is calculated in Table 3.4 and varies with the ability of the ACP exporters to fulfil their quotas; none having exhausted their quota in this period.

Averaged over the three year periods 1991-1993 and 1994-1996, St. Lucia experiences the greatest loss, at ECU 8.5 million per annum (m.p.a.), while Dominica (ECU 6.5m.p.a.), St. Vincent (ECU 6.7m.p.a.) and Jamaica (ECU 6.4m.p.a.) share a similar decline. Grenada, with its low volume of banana exports, loses the least at ECU 0.9m.p.a., while Belize's low losses at ECU 1.3m.p.a. result from a compensating rapid increase in the volume of exports, almost doubling between 1992 and 1996.

These annual loses can be contrasted not only with the allocations of SSA to individual ACP producers, but also with the total value of all EU aid during the ten years of Lomé IV. For Belize this totals ECU 11.5m., Jamaica ECU 77.5m., St. Lucia ECU 13m., St. Vincent ECU 12m., Dominica ECU 18.7m., and Grenada ECU 11.6m.

While the 1994 SSA was intended to provide compensation for the loss of national preferences with the adoption of the single market, the 1999 SSA (Regulation 856/1999) provided compensation for the phasing out of import licenses under the subsequent further reform of the Banana Protocol (see below). This current scheme allocates funds on the basis of the competitiveness gap of an ACP - the least competitive producers receiving the largest allocation - and the significance of banana production to the economy. It covers a longer period, ten years, and provides significantly larger sums of money, ECU 450m., allocated to twelve ACP producers. The Windward Islands are the principle beneficiary of this increased aid, receiving ECU 22m.p.a. The funds may also be used outside of the banana industry in order to diversify their economies.

Impact upon the EU Banana Market

The consequences of the adoption of the new Banana Regime for the EU banana market appears to have been much as would have been expected. With the introduction of the EU quota-tariff, imports declined from their 1992 peak of 3.4mt. to 3.18mt. in 1994. At the same time although the opening up of the UK and French markets to dollar imports reduced prices, in Germany the new regime appeared to raise prices by 48 per cent.

However care is needed in the interpretation of these figures. As has already been noted the pattern of imports in the early 1990s is likely to have been distorted by the dumping of bananas on the EU market by the US MNCs as they attempted to increase their market share in anticipation of the new regime. They correctly anticipated that any quota system would be based upon recent import figures. This particularly affected Germany by depressing prices to historically low levels. But this may have been offset to some degree by the dramatic increase in East Germany's per capita consumption with reunification - from 3.9kg. per capita in 1989 to 22.5kg. per capita in 1992 (cf. 14.6kg. per capita in West Germany). The combination of these two distorting effects is likely to have had a much greater impact upon German banana prices than the introduction of the more restrictive EU Banana Regime in 1993 (see Hallam and Peston 1997).

For the Caribbean Island producers problems had arisen even before the official adoption of the new Regime. It has been estimated that the break-even price for Windward Island bananas is ECU 586 per tonne (Gill and Gonzales 1995). Prices in the UK had begun to fall in September 1992, bottoming out at ECU 510 per tonne (c.i.f.) in January 1993. Subsequently they recovered to average ECU 601 per tonne in 1993 and ECU 622 per tonne in 1994. Unfortunately the price recovery coincided with a 15 per cent fall in sterling's value relative to the dollar, producing a 22 per cent fall in the price received by farmers. In response the Banana Growers Associations had to intervene to support prices. Nonetheless production had fallen 12.6 per cent by the end of 1993 and the Associations were running out of financial reserves.

Nor were the Windward Islands able to turn to the EU's Stabex fund for commodity support. Lomé IV had introduced a large element of conditionality into Stabex grants and abolished advanced payments before agreements were reached. Thus with prices hovering only just above their break-even level and the exhaustion of their financial reserves, the Windward Islands remained especially vulnerable to any further fall in EU prices.

Challenges to the Banana Regime

For the ACP producers the most important subsequent developments have been the challenges to the new Banana Regime mounted both within the Community and by the EU's trading partners. The German government and Benelux importers attempted to challenged the legality of this Regulation before the European Court, but without success. Also, as expected, the Latin American banana exporters initially requested the Protocols reference to the GATT panel. Only Guatemala pursued the objection and in early 1994 the GATT panel ruled against the Regime. In the face of opposition from the EU and ACP states the ruling could not be adopted by GATT. However within the context of the Uruguay Round negotiations Colombia, Costa Rica, Nicaragua and Venezuela arrived at a 'Framework Agreement' with the EU. This was intended to run until 2002 and increased the tariff-quota to 2.2m. tonnes and reduced the tariff to ECU 75 per tonne. Specific shares of the global quota were allocated to the four countries and in exchange they agreed not to raise any objection with the WTO until 2003.

Meanwhile in the US legal action had been taken under Article 301 of the Omnibus Trade Act, which requires the US government to identify those countries undertaking unfair trading practices and authorises unilateral retaliatory trade restrictions if they continue. The initial complaint was raised by the US multi-national Chiquita in association with the Hawaii Banana Producers Association. Hawaii produces very few bananas but it's involvement was necessary for the action to proceed. This initial case was terminated in September 1995.

But the greatest challenge to the new Regime was the complaint registered with the new World Trade Organisation in September 1995 by the United States and Honduras, Guatemala and Mexico (later joined by Ecuador). After attempts at conciliation failed a Disputes Settlement Body (DSB) panel was established in May 1996. In September 1997 the DSB report was adopted, finding that 'fundamental elements' were inconsistent with WTO obligations (for a detailed discussion of the WTO compatibility of the Banana Regime see Grynberg 1998). The report accepts the principle of preferential tariffs for ACP banana imports and supports the exemption of the Lomé Convention from the full force of WTO rules. WTO members had reaffirmed the exemption of Lomé until the year 2000 from observing Article 1 of GATT in October 1996. This Article requires the extension of any trade preference on a particular product to all WTO members (most-favoured-nation rule).

However the DSB ruled against the guarantee of 30 per cent of the

EU market for traditional ACP exporters ('B' Licenses which require the import of ACP bananas to obtain the right to import dollar bananas) and the differential treatment of banana imports from Colombia, Costa Rica, Nicaragua and Venezuela, compared with the rest of Latin America. These procedures were found to be in breach of Article XIII of GATT (concerning the non-discriminative administration of quantitative restrictions). The arrangements were also found to have breached Article II (most-favoured-nation treatment) and Article XVII (national treatment) in their impact upon banana industry service suppliers. It also criticises the size of the ACP quotas as being well above their maximum exports in the past.

Unlike GATT decisions the EU was obliged to accept the WTO rulings and in January 1998 the Commission responded with proposals for modifications to the Banana Regime that it believed would make it compatible with WTO requirements. The duty-free quota of imports from the ACP states would be maintained at 857,700 tonnes, but no longer allocated to any specific ACP countries. The MFN tariff quota of 2.2mt. for dollar and non-traditional ACP imports would also remain, with the dollar bananas continuing to pay a tariff of ECU 75 per tonne and the ACP fruit entering duty-free. The 353,000 tonnes addition to the tariff quota, which has been granted each year by the Management Committee to reflect the entry of Austria, Finland and Sweden, would become a permanent increase, with dollar banana paying a duty of ECU 300 per tonne and ACP non-traditional fruit ECU 100 per tonne. For imports above the tariff quota limit dollar bananas would face a tariff of ECU 765 per tonne and ACP fruit ECU 665 per tonne. The existing licensing system would be abolished and replaced with one that distinguishes between traditional suppliers to the EU market and new entrants - the latter's share of licenses increasing from 3.5 per cent to 8 per cent. These proposals maintain the overall value of the trade concessions offered to the ACP growers and avoids the threat of depressed prices through increasing the tariff-quota beyond the existing 2.2mt.

However the US and Ecuador rejected the new scheme as still being incompatible with the the EU's WTO obligations and lodged a further objection with the organisation. Further in January 1999 the US sought authorisation to introduce compensatory tariffs on $520 million of EU imports to bring the matter to a head. As a result the EU sought arbitration in the dispute by the WTO.

The EU had argued that a duty-free import quota for ACP bananas was exempt from WTO requirements under the Lomé waiver. However this had already been rejected by the WTO Appellate body and this view was reiterated in the Arbitrators' decision in April 1999 (see Sandiford for a detailed review of the Panel's ruling). The differential treatment of ACP suppliers, with access to a 857,700 tonne tariff quota, was again found to be in breach of Article XIII.1. This requires that no restriction should be applied by a WTO member state on the importation of any product of any other member state unless a similar restriction is applied to imports from all other countries. The Arbitrators also upheld the US objection to the size of the ACP quota. They observed that over the period 1994 to 1996, the years chosen by the EU to determine the 857,700 tonne quota, ACP imports had only totalled 685,000 tonnes. By contrast the MFN tariff quota of 2.2 million tonnes had already been reached. During this period the existing EU banana regime also distorted the share of imports provided by Colombia and Costa Rica. Therefore they ruled that the years 1994 to 1996 do not constitute a representative period upon which to base an allocation that meets the requirements of Art. XIII.2 – i.e. one that achieves 'a distribution of trade approaching as closely as possible the shares which various members might be expected to obtain in the absence of restrictions'.

Similarly in considering the revised licensing arrangements they again concluded that the carry-over effects of the previous regime, through the use of the 1994-1996 period as a basis for allocating licenses, gave EU/ACP operators an unfair advantage and that the new regime remained in breach of Art. XVII. However the Arbitrators reduced the volume of EU imports upon which the US could remove its tariff concessions to $192 million per annum.

A Final Settlement?

In May 1999 the EU Commission presented a Communication to the Council outlining three options for resolving the dispute. These were, moving to a flat rate tariff, removing the ACP preference while maintaining the overall 2.5m.t. tariff quota, or the introduction of a new tariff-rate quota. After further consultation it became clear that both the Latin American dollar producers and the ACP suppliers wished to maintain a tariff quota system, but there was no consensus as to the principles to be adopted in the allocation of the licences, which could well result in further action by both the US and Ecuador. In response in November the Commission proposed a two stage scheme (COM (1999) 582), with the retention of tariff quotas for a transitional period until January 2006 when a tariff-only regime would be adopted. During the initial phase the tariff quota of 2.5m.t. - 2.2m.t. 'A' quota, plus 353,000 'B' quota granted after EU enlargement - would be maintained, within which the ACP suppliers would continue to enjoy a zero tariff while Latin American producers would face a duty of €75p.t. However the zero-duty ACP quota of 850,000 t. ('C' quota) would be opened up to all suppliers, albeit with the imposition of an additional tariff of €275p.t. The method to be adopted for the distribution of import licenses remained open to negotiation, with both an historic basis and a 'first come, first served' (FCFS) being possibilities, however the Commission came to favour the latter. If no agreement could be reached the Commission proposed moving straight to the WTO compatible tariff-only regime.

For the ACP exporters the move from volume limits on imports to a tariff-only regime remained unacceptable. Although the EU had suggested a tariff of €275p.t. on non-ACP bananas, the general world surplus would result in a major increase in the quantity of EU imports, depressing prices in the European market. Although EU growers would continue to receive deficiency payments and the large international companies importing dollar bananas might be able to sustain short run losses, the high cost ACP producers were likely to be squeezed out of the market. These fears were effectively conveyed to the various policy makers within the Community. The European Parliament's response was to reject the proposal to move to a tariff only regime, call for maintenance of the tariff-quotas for at least 10 years and an ACP preference of €300p.t. Although one Spanish Parliamentarian referred to the Commission's proposals as 'agricultural genocide' for ACP banana producers, other voices were sympathetic to a transitional tariff-quota regime based upon the Commission's favoured FCFS.

But clear opposition also emerged from the nine Latin American producers, who at a meeting in August 2000 rejected the EU's proposals as sustaining unfair competition. Instead they expressed support for an alternative proposal emanating from the Caribbean exporters. This advocated the maintenance of the 2.7m.t. quota, with a common tariff regardless of source, together with an additional 850,000 t. quota for imports at a zero-tariff from the ACP states, with a higher tariff for other exporters. Most importantly it rejected FCFS in favour of the retention of quotas based upon historic trade. This scheme had already attracted the support of the US as a basis for negotiation.

But the Commission was by now firmly committed to the FCFS system for allocating import licences and in October the European General Affairs Council ratified the Commission's proposals, including FCFS. The new regime was to be introduced by April 2001, although the Commission could delay implementation until July 2001 in the event of administrative difficulties. As in the original proposal the 2.5m.t. ('A' and 'B' quotas) would have a tariff rate of €75p.t., with duty free access for the ACP suppliers. For the 850,000 t. 'C' quota non-ACP suppliers would face a duty increased from €275p.t., as initially proposed, to €300p.t., as advocated by the European Parliament. The three quotas were to be managed on a fortnightly or weekly basis and allocated to importers when their vessels were a specific distance from European ports. FCFS was seen by the Commission as offering a number of advantages. It was WTO compatible and recognised as a method of quota management, it was transparent and flexible, without requiring special management tools such as the definition of operators, and it removed the need to distinguish between traditional operators and new entrants. Agricultural Commissioner Franz Fischler regarded FCFS as offering what the Member States had asked for, 'a workable, WTO compatible system. FCFS is the key to putting an end to a dispute that has already gone on for too long'. His view was to prove optimistic.

Although the incoming US Bush administration appeared to be more sympathetic to FCFS, and indeed had advocated such an approach itself in the past, the ACP producers immediately rejected the new scheme. Meanwhile Chiquita Brands International, the world's largest banana producer and one of the principal instigators of the US action against the EU, was facing bankruptcy. It claimed that it had incurred losses of $200m. a year since 1992 as a result of the EU's restrictive banana regime.

By March 2001 the US opposition to FCFS had hardened and there was a threat of further US sanctions against EU exports. In turn there was a danger that the dispute would escalate, with the EU implementing retaliation against US exports, justified by the Foreign Sales Corporation tax scheme that the US had adopted, and which the EU opposed as an illegal export subsidy. The EU therefore agreed to suspend implementation of FCFS and resume negotiations with the US on their preferred historical reference system of import license allocation. However the 1st July remained the deadline for adoption of the new regime. EU Trade Commissioner Lamy noted that the EU 'would like to take some more time to look at how we can solve this dispute before we lock into FCFS'. Finally on the 11th April agreement was reached, with the EU conceding the allocation of licenses on the basis of 1994-1996 exports. The quotas were to be adjusted to expand the access for Latin American produce by reallocating approximately 100,000t. from the 'C' quota to 'A' and 'B'. The remaining 750,000t. of the 'C' quota being reserved exclusively for ACP producers. The US pledged to support the EU's request for a WTO waiver from the Art. 13 requirement for non-discrimination and, once granted, lift the trade sanctions it had imposed. Meanwhile the EU would be commencing negotiations with the WTO for the implementation of a tariff-only regime from the 1st January 2006.

The US Trade Representative, Franz Fischler, and the EU's Commissioner Lamy, regarded this agreement as the final act in a long saga and as marking 'a significant breakthrough...which will end the past friction and move us toward a better basis for the banana trade'. However the vexatious issue of the allocation of the quotas remained unresolved and almost immediately Ecuador, the largest Latin American exporter, sought discussions with the EU, having filed an official request with WTO Dispute Settlement Body. Ecuador believed that the new plan would disadvantage the majority of its national operators and was therefore seeking to retain a specific quota for new suppliers. But finally even Ecuador was satisfied, with the confirmation of the transfer of 100,000 t. from the 'C' quota and the abandonment of country quota allocations within the 2.6m.t. 'A' and 'B' quota. Having overcome the final obstacle the new regime came into effect from the 1st July 2001.

Adapting to Change?

By 1998 Belize's exports of bananas to the EU had almost doubled to 53m. tonnes (Table 3.5) and alone amongst the Caribbean ACP producers she had supplied up to the maximum available quota. By contrast, despite receiving prices almost double those of non-ACP exporters, the remaining island suppliers have dramatically reduced their exports. Jamaica has experienced the smallest fall of only 5m.t., but the Windward Island exporters have experienced an almost halving of their volumes; St. Lucia by 52m.t., St. Vincent by 32m.t. and Dominica by 24m.t. In St. Lucia half of all banana farmers ceased production between 1993 and 1997. Although all the Caribbean suppliers have substantially improved the quality of their fruit there remains a significant difference in the cost of supply. Precise figures remain difficult to establish but Windward Island bananas appear to cost 63 per cent more than Costa Rica bananas to produce (Hubbard, 2000).

Belize has the greatest potential to develop a competitive banana industry, although its costs remain higher than elsewhere in Central America. Productivity is already averaging 12.5 tonnes per acre. However there is a question mark over the contribution of the EU's SSA programme to this process. Although some of the investments in the infrastructure of the industry may yield benefits in time, there has been failure to identify clearly the main constraints upon increasing the competitiveness of the industry and to focus expenditure upon those areas (Hubbard, 2000). However the potential of Belize has already been recognised by the private sector, which has recently substantially increased its investment. The role of the EU's SSA may be more peripheral to the future of the industry than in other Caribbean ACP states, but the preferential quotas remain of crucial importance. Quota constraints resulted in 1,200 acres being taken out of cultivation in 1998-1999.

The position of Jamaica's banana industry is far less clear. How far the fall in exports reflects an underlying failure to improve competitiveness or the impact of natural disasters, especially hurricanes and crop disease, is difficult to determine. The EU's aid to the banana industry has concentrated upon the smaller growers, despite the larger estates offering the greatest prospect of increased productivity and competitiveness. These estates provide 70 per cent of Jamaica's exports and yield 15 tonnes per acre, compared with 3.4 tonnes per acre from the smaller independent growers. This orientation of EU assistance can be explained in part by the social impact of the contraction of the industry. The reduction in output and the drive for increased productivity has reduced employment to an estimated 4,000, with an additional 10,000 in supporting services. However the remaining employment is concentrated in particular areas - half of the 400 small banana producers are concentrated in one parish, Portland - and any reduction in employment must be seen in the context of the overall unemployment problem of Jamaica. But this in itself is only an argument for focusing funds on the creation of alternative economic activity in these areas.

The halving of the Windward Islands banana exports from a peak of 277,000 tonnes in 1990 to only 141,000 tonnes in 1998, has reflected the enhanced competition from dollar bananas and the hurricane damage of 1994 and 1995. The failure of the government controlled Banana Growers Associations (BGA) to provide commercial leadership has been a particular focus of criticism (Hubbard et al, 2000, Sandiford, 2000). Geest had taken a more indirect role in the marketing of Windward bananas and this, combined with the break-up of the larger estates, has left the Producers Associations in a pivotal role. With the assistance of aid donors, including the EU, the Windward Islands have been attempting to raise both productivity and quality (Sandiford, 2000). However this has exposed the weaknesses of the current marketing arrangements. Growers receive only 61 per cent of the f.o.b. value of their bananas from the BGAs compared with over 90 per cent in Jamaica and Belize, suggesting considerable inefficiency. The BGAs and the Windward Islands Banana

Development and Export Company (WIBDECO) had all faced cash flow and debt problems and had received EU funds to sustain them. In view of their failure to reform in 1997 the EU's technical assistance was shifted away from the BGAs and towards schemes to directly improve field productivity (e.g. St. Vincent irrigation project). But the current EU ACP quotas have forced Fyffes, through its subsidiary Geest (since 1995 a jointly owned company of Fyffes and WIBDECO) to continue to be involved in the Windward Islands banana industry. They have invested in the industry and put pressure on the governments to improve marketing. They strongly support the certification programme, which monitors the quality of the produce of small farmers and controls eligibility for assistance.

However the future strategy for the industry has yet to be agreed. Some critics advocate the retention of the statutory monopolies of the BGAs, but with the removal of cross subsidisation of the small and less productive growers. Others look to the example of St. Lucia where the BGA was privatised as the St. Lucia Banana Corporation (SLBC). However even this has not been without its continuing difficulties. As the SLBC is dominated by the smaller growers, with a one member one vote rule, the larger growers have formed a separate organisation, Total Quality Fruits. Privatisation of the WIBDECO joint venture with Fyffes (trading under the Geest name) that is responsible for shipping and ripening, has also been suggested, with WIBDECO concentrating upon a coordination role. Overall the abolition of the statutory marketing monopolies of the existing BGA and their replacement with voluntary Associations dominated by the strongest growers, and the competitive purchase of services by these Associations (including transport), is seen as the way forward (Hubbard, 2000).

But such institutional reforms in the Windwards fails to address the central issue of the long term competitiveness of their banana production in the event of a loss of tariff quota protection in the EU market. Although building upon the traditional UK market, with its preference for smaller sweeter bananas, and emphasising the 'fair trade' nature of their produce offers some potential to sustain their market share, a question mark still hangs over the long-term future of the industry in these islands. There is a danger that assistance to the banana industry, intended to enhance its competitiveness, may prove futile, but have induced continued investment by the smaller growers in the forlorn prospect of a sustainable future. The need for a greater emphasise upon diversification has been recognised in the focus of EU aid. All Stabex funds are now invested outside of the banana industry. Although bananas still represent 59 per cent of export earnings for St. Lucia, 51 per cent for Dominica and 33 per cent . Vincent (1997), even for these islands this is only 7 per cent, 7.4 per c and 6 per cent of GDP respectively. It is expected that structural change in the industry will result in a one third reduction in the number of growers in the next few years.

Conclusion

The changes to the EU banana market have been profound for a number of small and economically vulnerable Commonwealth Caribbean island economies. These changes have been driven by the requirements of the single European market, but even more by the demands of the WTO. A further opening up of the European banana market to dollar banana competition seems inevitable, with a consequent fall in prices.

To meet this challenge Stabex and SSA funds have been used to raise the productivity and improve the marketing of ACP bananas. In the Caribbean there are examples of SSA projects successfully raising productivity, through irrigation, drainage and replanting, and improving disease control and packing, but the future of the industry lies in a greater awareness of market requirements. Certification has been successful in enhancing quality control but may need to go further if these high cost producers are to exploit the niche for 'fair trade' or 'organic' produce. There needs to be a recognition of the dwindling importance of the wholesalers in the EU market and the emergence of the major supermarket retailers as the major players. The historic dominance of the international vertically integrated banana companies is likely to diminish in this new retail environment. It will be essential for the local Associations to respond to these market changes if their industry is to survive.

The EU's initial approach to assisting the ACP banana producers of the Caribbean adjust to the new trade regime assumed that they could achieve a sufficient improvement in their competitiveness to sustain a reasonable market share of the EU market. The Cotonou Agreement restates the EU's commitment to 'ensuring the continued viability of their (ACP) banana export industries and the continuing outlet for their bananas in the Community market' (Protocol 5 Art. 1) through measures to improve 'the conditions of the production and enhancement of quality through action in the areas of research, harvesting, packaging and handling; transport and storage; marketing and trade promotion' (Art. 2). While the EU can certainly contribute, through conditionality and technical assistance, to essential institutional reforms - in the Windwards reform of

ımaica changes in the plantation sector that address the
unrest and theft - the long term viability of much of the
uestioned. It is increasingly recognised that production
slands and amongst the smaller producers of Jamaica
nited long-term future. Thus an increasing emphasise is
ı diversification and this is most self-evident in the
funds.

However diversification for these island economies is not without its difficulties. Any attempt to diversify into alternate crops may be frustrated by the enhanced competition arising from a number of countries pursuing a similar strategy and entering the same commodity markets, or by changes in the world trade environment. The prospects for agricultural diversification are also highly dependent upon the continuation of the banana industry itself. This is particularly apparent when the industry's role in sustaining transport infrastructure is considered. The economic development of all small island economies is constrained by the high costs of transport. The existence of a regular 'reefer' banana shipping service from these islands to Europe allows the carriage of additional commodities at a low marginal cost, while also providing cheap return transport for 'back-loaded' imports (see Hallam and Peston 1997).

Development of the tourism or financial sectors is favoured in some development strategies. However international tourism is an unstable and highly competitive industry, with a high import dependence. While some islands have been particularly successful in developing their offshore financial industry these are now under threat from the requirements of the OECD and the inter-governmental Financial Action Task Force (FATF) to counter money laundering and tax evasion. These are seen as a sufficient threat to the long term future of these centres that CARICOM is challenging them before the WTO.

For Jamaica its larger economy may be able to absorb the adverse impact of any loss of EU market share. However for Dominica, St. Lucia and St. Vincent adjustment will prove much more difficult and their external status leaves them more vulnerable. As ACP mini-states their future may depend to a considerable degree upon the success of regional integration, which will be encouraged by the intended regional nature of the new economic partnership agreements with the EU. Ironically it is the Caribbean ACP members that have been most hostile to such regional agreements. The level of continuing political commitment by the UK government may be another crucial factor. Given that it was the UK that encouraged them to diversify out of sugar production and into bananas in the early 1970s, when the UK entered the EC, such a continuing concern might appear justified.

The challenge to the EU's Banana Regime before the new WTO has turned this issue into something of a 'cause celebre'. It has precipitated substantial discussion and analysis and raised a number of important issues. It has raised the question of the long-term future of the Lomé Convention and its compatibility with WTO obligations. It has focused attention on the failure of international agreements to address the role of large MNC oligopolists in international trade. As has been observed, the value of all ACP banana exports is equal to only 10 per cent of Chiquita's global earnings (Hallam and Peston 1997), and yet the WTO can only address the anti-competitive practices of countries not MNCs. It has highlighted the conflict between the EU's development and trade objectives and obligations and raised questions as to the substitutability of aid and trade. But in this general discussion there remains the danger that the serious implications of these developments for some of the smallest and most vulnerable ACP states may be lost.

References

Borrell, B. (1994), EU Bananarama III: Policy Research Working Paper No. 1386, World Bank.

Borrell, B. and Yang, M. C. (1990), EC Bananarama 1992: World Bank Working Papers in International Trade No. WPS 523.

Commission of the European Communities (1992), Proposal for a Council Regulation on the Common Organisation of the Market in Bananas: COM 359/92.

Commission of the European Communities (1992), Proposal for a Council Regulation (EEC) establishing a Special System of Assistance to Traditional ACP suppliers of Bananas: COM 465/92.

Davenport, M. and Page, S. (1991), *1992 and the Developing World*: Overseas Development Institute, London.

European Economic Community (1993), Council Regulation EEC/404/93.

FAO (1996), Effects of Policy Developments on Global Banana Trade: Committee on Commodity Problems, Intergovernmental Group on Bananas.

Flynn, G. (1992), Distribution, Europe's Banana Split: *Business and Finance* 28 (April).

Gill, H. and Gonazales, P. (1995), Economic Consequences of a Banana Collapse in the Caribbean: Report to the Caribbean Banana Exporters Association.

Grynberg R. (1998), The WTO incompatibility of the Lomé Convention trade provisions: Asia Pacific School of Economics and Management, Australian National University, SP 98/3.

Hallam, D. and Peston, M. (1997), The Political Economy of Europe's Banana Trade: University of Reading, Dept. of Agriculture and Food Economics, Occasional Paper No. 5.

Hubbard, M., Herbert, A. and Touche, Y. R. (2000), Evaluation of EU Assistance to ACP

Banana Producers, European Commission.

McInerney, J. and Peston, M. (1992), Fair trade in Bananas?: University of Exeter, Report No. 239.

Noich, A. (1985), European Community Trade Relations for Bananas and Imports from Developing Countries: *Quarterly Journal of International Agriculture*, 24.

Nurse, K. and Sandiford, W. (1995), *Windward Island Bananas: Challenges and Options under the Single European Market*, Friedrich Ebert Stiftung, Kingston.

Read, R. (1986), The Banana Industry: Oligopoly and Barriers to Entry in *Multinational and World Trade*, ed. M. Casson pp. 317-42, Allen & Unwin, London.

Read, R. (1994), Small Scale Banana Growers in the Windward Islands in *Poverty, Inequality and Rural Development*, ed. Lloyd, T. and Morrissey O., Macmillan, London.

Read, R. (1994b), The EC Internal Banana Market, The Issues and the Dilemma: *World Economy*, 17 (2, March) pp. 219-235.

Sandiford W. (2000), *On the Brink of Decline, Bananas in the Windward Islands*: Fedon Books, St. Georges, Grenada.

Thomas, M. (1989), Cash Crops and Development, Bananas in the Windward Islands: Institute of Development Studies Discussion Paper 258.

Thomas, M. (1989b), Agricultural Diversification, The Experience of the Windward Islands: Institute of Development Studies Discussion Paper 257.

World Bank (1994), Caribbean Region, Coping with Changes in the External Environment: Report No. 12821 LAC.

Yankey, B. (1993), The Possible Impact of a Banana Shock on the OECS Economies: Caribbean Development Bank.

4 From Insiders to Outsiders: Caribbean banana interests in the new international trading framework

PETER CLEGG

The history of the Commonwealth Caribbean banana export trade has been one underpinned by close political and economic ties with Europe, and particularly the United Kingdom. The development of the Jamaican trade at the turn of the twentieth century, and the establishment of the trade in the Windward Islands and Belize after the Second World War, were dependent on access to the United Kingdom market, and financial support from the British government. What followed was the creation of a tightly knit relationship between the main actors involved in exporting Caribbean bananas to the United Kingdom, including the banana producers, the private corporate interests, and the relevant UK government departments. Indeed there was evidence that a degree of clientelism existed, whereby the government departments who had dealings with the Caribbean banana interests identified with their concerns and policy objectives. The close relationship between the actors in question was institutionalised with the creation of the Banana Advisory Committee in 1973 which oversaw banana imports into the UK, and the fundamental strength of this relationship was sustained when the UK first entered the European Economic Community (EEC) in 1973. Due to the highly divergent nature of EEC member states banana import regimes, the UK was able to maintain its particular banana policies on accession, and to continue its colonial and post-colonial trading relationships. However, from the mid-1980s the close ties that existed between the Caribbean banana interests and the UK government began to be challenged on a number of fronts. This chapter considers these challenges and argues that the national and regional commitments to retain long term trading patterns have now been superseded by the institutional nature of the newly created international trading environment, overseen by the World Trade Organisation.

The Rationale for a European Single Market

In the early 1980s, there was a belief amongst those in the European corridors of power that inefficiencies resulting from trade barriers between member states were causing the Community to lose ground with the competing economies of Japan and the United States. As a consequence, the European Commission published a white paper in 1985 laying out the basis for a more integrated trading structure, which underpinned the subsequent negotiations between the member states of the Community. Through the efforts of all those involved, the Single European Act (SEA) was signed in February 1986, and enacted in July 1987. The objective of the SEA was to achieve a single market by 31st December 1992.

One of the tasks committed to under the SEA was the elimination of internal frontier controls, which required the introduction of common rules to govern trading relations with third countries. In essence, member states would no longer be able to unilaterally decide whether to place restrictions on, or provide preferential treatment for, goods that originated outside of the Community. Thus in order for individual member states to continue their particular trade policies they had to persuade fellow member states and the Commission to adopt European-wide measures that satisfied their trading requirements. The importation of bananas was one area of trade policy where the member states were completely at variance with the ideals of the single market. Bananas were one of the few agricultural products not yet covered by Community rules, neither being subject to the Common Agricultural Policy, or in reality the Common Commercial Policy with the 20 per cent tariff-only being effective in certain member states.

When the Single European Act was passed there were three distinct banana regimes:

- a preferential market for EC/ACP produced bananas in Britain, France, Greece, Italy, Portugal, and Spain;
- a duty-free market in Germany, and
- a market subject to a 20 per cent tariff in Belgium, Denmark, Ireland, Luxembourg, and the Netherlands.

Within the context of a single market the continuation of national regimes was unsustainable, but due to the respective obligations on the part of member states to their banana suppliers, and the difference in production costs between Latin American banana imports (0.200 ECU/kg), and ACP/EC banana imports (0.500 ECU/kg), there was no single market arrangement that was readily acceptable to every member state (Pedler, 1995, p. 72). Any free market solution would have undoubtedly been to the benefit of the US multinational companies, dealing in dollar bananas, while those companies dealing in ACP and EC fruit would have suffered. However, a too restrictive European banana regime would not have encouraged greater competitiveness and efficiency in the market, a fundamental aim of the single market. Thus the problem came down to finding a market mechanism which safeguarded the position of the ACP/EC suppliers, while encouraging some degree of competition within the market.

The Construction of Coalitions of Interest

Despite the important ramifications of a single market for the preferred banana producers, particularly those of the Commonwealth Caribbean, the governments and grower organisations of these countries were rather complacent about its possible effects. Indeed, it took the banana marketing companies, the West India Committee, and certain interested individuals within the UK to alert the Caribbean to the possible consequences of a single European banana market.

By 1988, however, there was a general appreciation of the important developments within the EC, and as a result the Caribbean Banana Exporters Association (CBEA) was established to act as a political lobbying entity to influence the developing debate on the future European banana regime. The Association had as its members seven independent Caribbean banana producing countries of Jamaica, Dominica, Grenada, St. Lucia, St. Vincent, Belize and Suriname, with their respective banana marketing companies of Fyffes, Geest, and Jamaica Producers having associate status, supported by a public relations agency recruited to coordinate the lobbying effort. There was close cooperation between the banana growers and the marketing companies, as each group had an interest in sustaining preferential access in any future regime. Despite the historical differences between and within the various interests involved in the Caribbean banana trade, there was a realisation that if a united effort was not undertaken to safeguard the concept of preferential access in the forthcoming single market, their mutually respective interests could be damaged.

However, some members of the CBEA took a greater role in the lobbying process than others. In order to build the strongest argument for continued preferential access it was decided that the Windward Islands should take centre stage. This was because the Windward Islands were the most dependent of all the Caribbean producers on banana exports for their economic welfare, and the islands had the greatest predominance of small banana farmers, a situation which could be favourably compared with the large scale Latin American production. If Jamaica or Belize had been used to promote the case for Caribbean banana exports, then the arguments for retaining preferential access would have had less weight. Both countries have larger estate systems, based on the Latin American model, and their overall dependency on the banana crop is less than that for the Windward Islands.

Due to the emphasis on the Windward Islands, the Geest company, in classical lobby terms was in a strong position, and played a crucial role in arguing for the retention of preferential access in the new regime. Conversely, Fyffes was not at the forefront of the lobbying process as it was felt that because the company had just been sold by United Brands (formerly the United Fruit Company), that company's poor reputation would likely hinder the lobbying effort. Also, Fyffes was the major importer of dollar bananas into the UK, and it was thought unwise for such a company to be centrally involved in defending continued preferential access for Caribbean bananas. In addition, there was some suspicion on the part of the ACP over Fyffes' intentions because of its involvement in shipping bananas from the Dominican Republic to Europe after the Republic became party to the Fourth Lomé Convention, which was seen by the Commonwealth Caribbean as a threat to its own bananas exports.

There was also cooperation in the lobbying effort between the Caribbean, African and European Community banana producers. In the early stages of the process, overtures were made by the Association of European Banana Producers (AEBP) to the Caribbean, in an astute political move led by the French. There was a realisation that if the position of ACP bananas in the EC market was undermined in anyway, the arguments for continued support for EC production would be weakened. The French producers, therefore, believed that it made sense to associate themselves with the Windward Islands, as the political case for continued preferential access was the Windward Islands case. The French hoped that as the Windward Islands, Martinique, and Guadeloupe were geographical neighbours, comparisons would be made between them in terms of their dependency on banana exports, even though in reality their economic circumstances were quite different. However, it has to be stressed that despite this cooperation, the EC producers were ultimately only concerned with their own welfare.

The African countries, meanwhile, were also quite willing to let the Caribbean take the lead, while providing support when necessary. Again this was because the arguments that were to be used for continued preferential access were based on the methods of production in the Windward Islands; banana production in West Africa was conducted on a much larger scale. In addition, the Caribbean and African producers were represented on the ACP's banana group, which being based in Brussels, was able to keep in close contact with the European Commission, the Council of Ministers and the member states to make sure that any proposal suggested for the single market reflected the ACP's position. However, there were criticisms that as the ACP Secretariat was understaffed, those in the Caribbean lobby had to provide the impetus for ACP involvement in the process. Nevertheless, the establishment of an integrated lobbying framework meant that those forces defending the concept of preferential access were well placed to oversee the formulation of policy.

The task of designing suitable proposals for a single market in bananas was undertaken by the European Commission, in the guise of an Inter-Services Group established in 1988, involving a number of different Directorates-General, including those of Agriculture, Development and External Relations. Under such circumstances the CBEA/ACP lobby kept abreast of developments within the Commission, but also in order to make sure that the Commission did not take the initiative completely, made attempts to promote a wider political debate within the other institutions of the EC. In 1990, for example, the CBEA lobbied for and achieved an 'own initiative' opinion in the European Parliament which supported continued preferential access for ACP/EC producers. The Parliament took the subject up long before the Commission had formulated a proposal, and in doing so it meant that the Commission would be obliged to accommodate the Parliament's view in some form. In a similar vein the Economic and Social Committee's (ECOSOC) Section for Agriculture and Fisheries produced an Information Report in 1991, which generally shared the European Parliament's view. The CBEA recognised from an early stage the importance of the different institutions of the EC, and that each institution had a crucial role to play in the policy formulation process. The initiation of investigations by both the European Parliament and ECOSOC provided the lobby in favour of retaining preferential access for certain banana producers with a strong base of support which the Commission was obliged to recognise.

The Importance of the Banana Protocol in the Fourth Lomé Convention

As the details of the single market in bananas had yet to be agreed, the ACP and the CBEA knew it was crucial that the Banana Protocol of the Lomé Convention should continue in its existing form. The undertaking in Article One of the protocol, 'As regards its exports of bananas to the markets of the Community, no ACP state will be placed, as regards access to its traditional markets and its advantages on those markets, in a less favourable situation than in the past or at present' (The Courier, January-February 1985, p. 111), was seen as vital in committing the EC to uphold the interests of the ACP banana producers in any single market proposal.

The negotiations for renewing the Lomé Convention began at the ACP/EC Council of Ministers meeting held in Brussels during October 1988. It was here that the first official Caribbean initiative on the banana issue was taken. The Prime Minister of Dominica, Dame Eugenia Charles, made representations to the Council seeking to have the Banana Protocol maintained in Lomé IV without adjustments. Further, at an ACP-EEC Joint Assembly meeting in Bridgetown in January 1989, a resolution was passed re-emphasising the special position of ACP banana exports, and the importance of the Banana Protocol in the Lomé Convention (Official Journal of the European Communities, 1989). A number of EC member states also recognised the importance of the Lomé Convention in setting the framework for future discussions on the banana issue, with the UK and France being particularly supportive of the ACP position. The German government, meanwhile, with some support from the Benelux countries, attempted to dilute the commitment of Article One of the protocol, believing that the ACP were not viable producers, and that they should instead receive compensation payments for diversification. The importance of the Banana Protocol lay in the fact that it was a legally binding commitment on the part of the EC to help safeguard market access for ACP banana producers, and thus the outcome of the renegotiation discussions would help determine the nature of the single market regime when it came.

Despite the opposition from some member states there was a critical mass of support for the protocol to be retained in its existing form. Although, the European Commission demanded and subsequently secured an attached declaration to the Lomé Convention, which re-stated its commitment to introduce a single market in bananas, fearing that without such a declaration the aims of the Single European Act as it applied to bananas would be compromised (Annex LXXIV, Joint declaration relating to Protocol 5, Fourth Lomé Convention, The Courier, January-February 1996, pp. 193-194). The Fourth Lomé Convention was signed in December 1989, and took effect the following March. The importance for the ACP of an unchanged Banana Protocol cannot be overstated. The various groups with an interest in sustaining the protocol had invested a great deal of time and energy in persuading member states and the European Commission to its point of view. The ACP/CBEA believed that no matter what kind of single market proposal on bananas was finally arrived at, the EC was bound by its legal commitments under the protocol. The securing of an unchanged Banana Protocol was important as it illustrated the ACP/CBEA's recognition of the inter-linked nature of the policy-making process of the EC. Further, there was an appreciation that a long-term approach was needed when attempting to influence policy, as the deadline for the introduction of a single market regime was still three years away.

A Comparison of Lobbying Approaches: Complacency versus Active Engagement

Although the commitment on the part of the EC to sustain ACP banana supplies in a single market was apparent, the exact method by which this would be done was still unclear. Therefore, all those actors with an interest in the banana trade still had an opportunity to shape the precise nature of the proposals. Within this context a number of member states undertook studies setting out their preferred single market options. The UK and France, for example, consistently supported proposals that would give clear guarantees to their preferential sources of supply, although they disagreed over the extent of market intervention that would be required to safeguard their traditional suppliers' place in the market. While the Benelux countries produced a document which strongly supported a liberalised banana market regime (Caribbean Banana Exporters Association, 1990; ACP Secretariat, 1991; Benelux Economic Union, 1991).

The principles of the UK position were set very early on when in July 1987, the then Prime Minister Margaret Thatcher, on a visit to Jamaica stated that, 'We shall continue to fight hard in the European Community, and we have quite a bit of experience of fighting in that organisation, to make sure that Jamaica and other Caribbean countries go on enjoying the preferential arrangements for bananas under the Lomé Convention' (Select Committee on Agriculture, 1992, p. 141). The Prime Minister was generally supportive because of her close relationship with the Dominica Prime Minister Dame Eugenia Charles, and because she was persuaded that the interests of the small island states should not be neglected by her government. It is important to recognise that despite the fact that Margaret Thatcher's economic beliefs were firmly based on market liberalisation, wider political and personal commitments were strong enough to override the Prime Minister's natural predilections. In addition, it was clear that there was some residual guilt within government circles that the legacy of colonial rule had led to the existing difficult set of circumstances for the Caribbean, and that the government had some responsibility to assist the islands during this period of uncertainty.

UK guilt

Although, the UK government's position seemed to be generally supportive of the ACP, the Caribbean lobby was determined to keep the pressure on, believing that the UK would be their strongest advocate in the Council of Ministers. As a consequence, an extensive lobbying campaign was undertaken both within government and parliamentary circles by the CBEA, with the assistance of its Parliamentary adviser, Bowen Wells, Conservative MP for Hertford and Stortford. Those interests within the UK banana trade that were in favour of a more 'liberal' single market solution, including the supermarkets and many of the independent banana importing and distributing companies, also undertook a lobby campaign, represented in parliament by Michael Jopling, then Conservative MP for Westmoreland and Lonsdale. However, those interests in favour of a more 'liberal' approach found only limited support within government and parliament, as there was an underlying sympathy for the Caribbean banana exporters in the UK. Despite the fact that there was a large Conservative majority in the House of Commons that supported an agenda which called for greater trade liberalisation, the particular circumstances of the banana issue transcended such considerations. The historical ties between the UK and the Caribbean, and the fact that the UK authorities had assisted the banana industry in the Caribbean over many years, were important considerations in determining the extent of support for the Caribbean banana producers within the UK body politic. It can also be argued that the extent of support for the Caribbean was underpinned by a paternalistic attitude on the part of some within the Conservative Party in particular, who felt that the UK should still have a role in overseeing the welfare of its former colonies.

within UK

Elsewhere in Europe the Caribbean lobby attempted to influence opinion in any way it could. The Prime Ministers of the Caribbean islands visited various member states, supported in their efforts by those at lower ministerial level. Attempts were also made to sensitise political opinion in the European Parliament, as it was hoped that an awareness of the ACP position would filter back to the member states. Further, a lobbying mission was undertaken by a Surinamese delegation to the Netherlands, while the existing links Geest had in Italy were also utilised. There was also a public relations campaign focussing on a number of publications, particularly those of the Financial Times and the Economist, which were perceived to be the most influential across Europe. In addition, the ACP Working Group on bananas published a memorandum, in November 1990, on its preferred option for a single market in bananas, and the West India Committee also published proposals, and organised conferences to acquaint opinion formers of the issues involved in the single market. All these activities on the part of the ACP lobby were intended to increase awareness of the arguments in defence of preferential access at all levels of society within the EC.

The forces supporting the ACP/EC banana producers had therefore been active both at the national and European levels for a considerable period of time. However, those interests that were in favour of a more liberal approach had in comparison badly misjudged the dynamics of the policy making process, believing wrongly that the liberalizing influences of the ongoing GATT negotiations, together with the Single European Act, would deliver a regime that was favourable to them. Although the American owned multinationals of United Brands and Dole hired leading lobbyists and trade lawyers in Washington and Brussels, and the Latin American producing countries organised visits to Europe, their campaigns came too late for them to have a significant effect on the formulation of policy. The European companies that imported and distributed dollar bananas were also late in realising the mood within the European institutions, a situation compounded by the fact that the Northern European countries in favour of a liberal regime, such as Germany, Holland, and Denmark were rather complacent when it came to pushing their preferred option for reform. However, it can be argued that for the liberal interests the banana issue was not a matter of faith as it was for the ACP/EC, and as a result did not have the same commitment as those groups supporting a preferential solution. The ACP/EC interests had much more to lose than the liberal interests had to gain from a single market, and so were absolutely determined to make sure all aspects of the policy-making process were covered. Further, the liberal interests never took the trouble to understand the approach taken by the Caribbean, and their rationale for doing so, while the Caribbean could not believe that the liberal interests were being so complacent.

The Issue of Tariffication: The Dunkel Compromise and the Shadow of GATT

After almost three years of discussion, the Inter-Services Group had formed a degree of consensus regarding proposals for a single market regime in bananas. In the Autumn of 1991, the group circulated proposals that indicated support for a quota system for dollar banana imports and a requirement to encourage the marketing companies to deal in Community and ACP bananas. The European Commissioners were then preparing to put forward their proposals when the GATT Secretary-General Arthur Dunkel introduced a new factor into the discussions in December 1991, by suggesting that bananas be included under the provisions of GATT. Some measure of agreement had been reached in the Uruguay Round on market access for tropical products in late 1988, but bananas had been explicitly excluded at the behest of the EC. Dunkel produced his compromise in an attempt to solve the wider problems surrounding agriculture in the Uruguay Round negotiations. He proposed that any restrictions on agricultural trade that had been underpinned by quotas should be replaced by tariffs, which could then be progressively reduced over time. The GATT Secretary-General's intervention went against what had been suggested by the Inter-Services Group, and as a consequence the European Commission felt it necessary to reassess its proposal. The intervention of the Secretary-General of GATT was important as it for the first time linked the development of a single market in bananas to the wider Uruguay Round trade negotiations that were entering their final phase. Although the GATT had shown an interest in the banana issue in the past, the intervention by Dunkel was significant in that it initiated the beginning of a period in which the body for world trade was to have a more influential role in determining the nature of the EC's banana import policy, and which in time was to supersede the traditional Caribbean banana producing interests.

After an intensive period of lobbying, during which time the ACP interests argued for the removal of bananas from the Dunkel compromise, a position supported by the ACP-EEC Joint Assembly and the European Parliament, the Commissioners attempted to determine the approach by which a draft regulation would be constructed. However, there were deep divisions amongst the Commissioners over the issue, and it was only after much heated discussion that they decided to endorse in principle the quota option with a complementary customs duty, to rule out Dunkel's proposal as a way forward, and to support the removal of bananas from the GATT negotiations (Caribbean Insight, May 1992).

In May 1992 a more substantive and detailed report was produced by the European Commission, which suggested that the quota for dollar bananas should be 1.4 million tonnes, subject to a bound customs rate of 20 per cent, and that an autonomous quota in association with a partnership scheme should be introduced to encourage all importers to become involved in the marketing of ACP/EC bananas (Commission of the European Communities, 1992a). Following the report, the Commission consulted representatives of the member states, producers and traders in the Community, and the banana exporting countries in the ACP and in Latin America. However, not all the interested parties were happy with the proposals, with the Latin American banana producing countries being particularly critical.

As a consequence in June 1992, Costa Rica, Colombia, Guatemala, Nicaragua and Venezuela opened consultations with the EC on whether the existing national banana regimes within the Community were GATT compatible. Other Latin American producers, such as Ecuador, who were also against the EC's proposals, were unable to participate in the action as they were not members of GATT, while the United States and the multinational banana companies were biding their time, waiting to see how their interests could best be served in the circumstances. The move to begin consultations at GATT was highly significant, as it was the first indication that the Latin American countries, in particular, had realised that their lobbying efforts had been unsuccessful, and alternative means to challenge the EC over bananas were needed. By challenging the existing national regimes of the Community, the Latin American countries hoped that this would set the scene for a challenge to the forthcoming single market regime, if it proved unacceptable to them.

The Formal Single Market Proposal and the Return of Tariffication

The assumption of the Presidency of the Council of Ministers by the UK in July 1992, meant that it had the responsibility of finding a solution to the banana issue that would be acceptable to the Council. Although agreement within six months, the length of each EC presidency, was not going to be easy, the Ministry of Agriculture was determined to find a settlement within that time. It was concerned that the two countries to follow the UK as President, Denmark and Belgium, would be less inclined to uphold the EC's obligations under the Lomé Convention. The Ministry of Agriculture believed that the UK had a responsibility to its traditional suppliers in the Caribbean, a commitment shared by John Gummer, the Minister of Agriculture, who believed the issues at stake went far wider than purely economic considerations. The Minister believed that the EC had a moral obligation to protect ACP, and particularly Caribbean banana growers, against the powerful US multinationals. Support was also forthcoming from the Prime Minister, John Major who had a close friendship with Sir James Mitchell, Prime Minister of St. Vincent. The efforts of the London based politicians and officials were supported by the UK Permanent Representation to the EC (UKREP) which acted as a contact point between Whitehall and the institutions of the EC. UKREP which had within it a number of officials dealing with agricultural matters, was vital in coordinating attempts to find an acceptable solution to the banana issue.

Despite deep divisions within the Council of Ministers, the body which would finally decide on the regime to be adopted, the European Commission published a 'Proposal for a EEC Council Regulation on the common organisation of the market in bananas', on 7th August. The formula suggested by the Commission was a compromise between Commissioners, aimed at meeting some of the concerns expressed by Latin American banana exporting countries that the proposed regime was too restrictive. Nevertheless the draft proposal issued leaned in favour of the ACP and EC producers, as had previous discussion documents, with no concessions on tariffication. It was also decided that any resolution of the single market issue should be framed with reference to Articles 42 and 43 of the Treaty of Rome, which meant that the decision would be taken under qualified majority voting, and that a degree of flexibility would be allowed in terms of what was required from a common banana policy (Rudden and Wyatt, 1980, pp. 34-37, and Commission of the European Communities, 1992b).

The essence of the Commission proposal was to give free entry to ACP and EC bananas, to place an absolute limit on the entry of Latin American bananas via a quota of 2 million tonnes (20 per cent customs duty), with an additional quota if EC consumption increased, and to encourage all banana importers to trade in ACP/EC bananas through a 'partnership' scheme involving 30 per cent of the dollar quota (Commission of the European Communities, 1992b). Although the Commission proposal was generally favourable to the ACP/EC position, it is important to recognise that the proposal was altered from its previous draft, adopting some of the recommendations suggested by the Latin American banana exporting interests. Therefore even though it seemed that the ACP/EC interests were in the ascendancy, there was still a degree of fluidity in the lobbying process.

After the Commission published its draft document in August the issue was considered in the Committee of Permanent Representatives (COREPER) and the Special Committee for Agriculture. Although attempts were made to narrow the differences between the member states, the entrenched positions on all sides remained and little progress was made. When the issue was sent to the November Agriculture Council meeting for further discussion, the divisions between the member states came to a head when those countries opposed to the Commission's proposal used their blocking majority and refused to even open negotiations on it. As a consequence, the UK Presidency was convinced that to break the deadlock a new approach was needed. The Minister of State at the Ministry of Agriculture, David Curry explained the situation, 'the UK presidency has done everything that it can to give that (Commission) proposal a fair wind. We have promoted it and given it wide debate'. Curry continued, 'The proposal is deadlocked in Brussels and does not have majority support. We have done the best that we can, but a group of Member States forming more than a blocking minority simply will not have it. We must therefore find a way out, and that falls to the Presidency' (European Standing Committee, 1992, p. 3).

The Ministry of Agriculture, in association with UKREP, therefore began work with the European Commission to amend the proposal. It was hoped that the changes would provide the basis for an agreement at the December Council meeting. An indication of the way forward can be seen when David Curry argued, 'the Dunkel text (tariffication) provides richer opportunities than we thought for effective protection for ACP and Community fruit' (European Standing Committee, 1992, p. 4). The work to amend the Commission proposal was therefore to be based on tariffication, despite the fact that the concept had been rejected earlier in the year. As the deadline for agreement was approaching, a solution had to be found, and the idea of tariffication was widely known. Therefore there was a pre-existing base of knowledge regarding the concept which it was hoped would allow a solution to be found in the time available. In addition work was undertaken by the Ministry and the Commission to formulate interim measures for the operation of the EC banana market beyond the end of December, if the details of a hoped for agreement were not in place by 1st January 1993. Such measures were designed to safeguard the ACP/EC banana suppliers place in the market, between the end of the old national regimes on 1st January and the introduction of the new regime whenever that came (Official Journal of the European Communities, 1993a).

While work was being undertaken on the amended proposal and the interim measures, John Gummer visited Jamaica and St. Lucia at the beginning of December 1992 to meet with Caribbean leaders, and the representatives of the respective banana industries. Publicly his trip was seen as an opportunity to inform those in the Caribbean about the framework of the new strategy and to reassure the islands that the new proposals would safeguard Caribbean banana producing interests; although privately it was said that the visit was an attempt to fend off more lobbying missions to Europe from Caribbean leaders, the cause of some embarrassment to the UK (Caribbean Insight, January 1993). However, it was apparent that the Caribbean countries were working closely with the Ministry on suitable amendments, despite the fact that tariffication was not their preferred option. On the size of the dollar quota, Curry stated that, 'the Caribbean countries have given us some parameters of what would be acceptable and what would be bearable, and clearly that will inform us in the discussions' (European Standing Committee, 1992, p. 10). It is important to recognise the close working relationship between the Caribbean banana interests and the UK government in designing a new proposal, illustrating the nature of the relationship that existed between them during this period of highly pressurised policy making.

Further, due to the particular EC policy making procedures, both the European Parliament and the Economic and Social Committee (ECOSOC) were involved in the consultation process. Although their remit was to consider the original Commission proposal, the Parliament and ECOSOC also took an interest in the process of amendment that was being undertaken by the UK government and the Commission. Due to the nature of the original proposal, the Parliament's Committee on Agriculture, Fisheries and Rural Development gave its opinion, although comment was also passed by the Committee on Budgets and the Committee on Development and Cooperation. The Committee on Agriculture was generally supportive of the Commission's proposal, although after significant ACP lobbying the Committee suggested that the reference period for 'traditional' banana imports from ACP states should be the best year prior to 1991, rather than solely 1990 as the Commission suggested. The ACP were concerned that the guaranteed volume of 620,000 tonnes per annum did not adequately take account of the expected increases in ACP banana production. In addition there was an attempt by two British Conservative MEPs, in cooperation with the UK government, to introduce an amendment promoting 'dirty tariffication', a mixture of tariff quotas for

ACP and dollar bananas and high over quota tariffs. Such an arrangement was being worked on by the UK government in an effort to break the deadlock in the Council of Ministers. Although, the amendment was ultimately unsuccessful there were indications that the concept of 'dirty tariffication' might be acceptable to a majority of member states in the Council (Official Journal of the European Communities, 1993c).

As in the Parliament, ECOSOC's section for Agriculture and Fisheries generally approved of the Commission's original proposal, although the reference period for 'traditional' banana imports from the ACP was criticised. Indeed the interests of the Caribbean banana producers appeared to be well represented, with the opinion of the Committee drafted by Ovide Etienne from Guadeloupe, while the Employers' Group had as its expert on the Committee, the Secretary of the Caribbean Banana Exporters Association (Official Journal of the European Communities, 1993b). Once again the importance of the other institutions of the EC in helping to shape ideas that could be adopted by the Member States should be recognised. Both the Parliament and ECOSOC acted as arenas of discussion which helped to determine the nature of the new proposals that the Commission and the UK government were working on, and it is significant that both institutions reaffirmed their support for the ACP/EC position.

A meeting of the Council of Agriculture Ministers was convened on the 14th December, at which John Gummer presented an outline compromise. Although the details of the amended proposal were significantly different to those of the Commission's original proposal, the underlying commitment remained the same, to preserve market access for EC and ACP bananas. There were three main elements to the amended proposal. There was an undertaking to provide tariff-free entry for traditional quantities of ACP bananas on a country specific basis, in any year up to and including 1990, instead of just 1990. For the EC producers there was provision for financial support and restructuring schemes, although banana production for the region was effectively capped at 854,000 tonnes. The proposal also called for the introduction of a fixed quota of 2 million tonnes for non-ACP/EC bananas at a tariff rate of ECU 100 per tonne (approximately 20 per cent), and the imposition of a ECU 850 (170 per cent) per tonne tariff on imports above that level. This was a change from the original Commission proposal which had purely quantitative restrictions on dollar bananas. Further, there was a commitment to introduce a system for the allocation of the dollar quota so that 30 per cent of the licences went to importers of ACP/EC bananas, allowing them to cross subsidise their operations with more profitable dollar fruit. This was a change from the draft proposal, since instead of 30 per cent being reserved for partnership arrangements, as was originally proposed, it was to be given in its entirety and unconditionally to traditional importers of ACP and EC bananas. The amended proposal thus went some way towards meeting what had been set out in the Dunkel Compromise the previous year, in that quotas should be replaced by tariffs. Indeed the principles of the new regime were incorporated into the agreement on agriculture between the EC and the United States within the context of the GATT Uruguay Round negotiations. When the amended proposal was presented the Commission and the UK government hoped that it would both be acceptable to enough member states for it to be adopted in Council, and would satisfy those interests outside the EC which had been critical of the original proposal.

The Final Negotiations and Eventual Agreement

When the amended proposal was put to the Council in mid-December it was positively received by most Member States, although Germany, Belgium, the Netherlands, and Denmark remained opposed, and would have had sufficient votes to form a blocking minority. However, a successful attempt was made by the UK Presidency to weaken the resistance to the proposal by placing the banana compromise in a wider package of measures that was to be voted on at this, the final Agriculture Council meeting of its Presidency. As the package had to be accepted or rejected in its entirety, the UK made sure that every member state had a reason to vote for it, even though they might have disagreed with the banana part of the package. The decision to place the revised banana proposal within a broader package of measures assisted considerably in reaching an agreement, with both Belgium and the Netherlands finally voting in favour, thus allowing the package to be adopted through a qualified majority.

Though the compromise on bananas was substantially different from the Commission proposal, the European Commissioner for Agriculture Ray McSharry chose to accept it. The President of the Council John Gummer, claimed that the proposal was 'wholly acceptable to all as it would safeguard the interests of ACP producers and protect the interests of EC banana producers, whilst being compatible with the Uruguay Round of free trade talks in the GATT'. He added, 'Small, vulnerable democratic nations like Jamaica and St. Lucia will have access to their traditional EC market whilst having a real opportunity to grow and compete' (Europe/Caribbean Confidential, 17 December 1992).

Usually with a compromise package at the end of a Presidency, all the legal texts are signed and sealed on the day of their agreement. However, for the banana issue, because of its controversial nature, there was no legal text. There was a Commission proposal, and a four page compromise on what was planned, but there was no legal form to the commitments. As a consequence between December and February there were discussions over what should be included in the legal text. In essence, December's vote had only established the principle of the regime, agreement over its detailed application still had to be decided. As it was the end of the UK's Presidency of the Council the responsibility for securing a vote on the detailed application of the banana proposal passed to Denmark, who had voted against the package in December. However, despite unprecedented behaviour by a number of Member States in withdrawing their support for what had been accepted two months before, a final agreement was reached at the February meeting, although only with the support of Denmark who was obliged to defend the integrity of EC procedures by supporting measures which had already been agreed in substance. The legal text and the internal aspects of the December council decision on the single banana regime were adopted on 12th February 1993 as Regulation 404/93 (Official Journal of the European Communities, 1993d). The common organisation of the market in bananas came into operation on 1st July 1993, and was due to last until 2002 (Official Journal of the European Communities, 1993e). The final adoption of a single market in bananas brought to an end almost six years of high level political activity on the part of the Caribbean banana interests to secure their objectives of sustaining a preferential market for their produce. However success was short lived, as greater and more fundamental challenges were soon threatening the legal basis on which the regime had been agreed.

The First Challenges to the Common Market in Bananas

Once the common market organisation in bananas had been agreed within the Council of Ministers, those forces that had been pushing for a 'liberal' regime began to explore other avenues of opposition. In May 1993, for example, Germany supported by Belgium and the Netherlands filed an unsuccessful complaint with the European Court of Justice requesting the annulment of the Council Regulation 404/93 (Official Journal of the European Communities, 1993f; Official Journal of the European Communities, 1993g; and Caribbean Insight, August 1993). Indeed, despite the fact that numerous court cases have been brought against the banana regime, the European Court of Justice has never ruled against the fundamental principles underpinning it. However other legal avenues have proved much more effective in undermining the political compromise achieved in the Council of Ministers.

The consequence of the five Latin American banana producing countries opening consultations with the EC in the GATT, in June 1992, over the whether the Community's national regimes were GATT compatible, was the establishment, eight months later, of a GATT Panel to formally consider the complaint. During the panel procedure, the ACP countries were represented by Jamaica, Cameroon, Ivory Coast, Senegal, and Madagascar. Significantly the Windward Islands were unable to participate directly, since they were not members of GATT. Nevertheless there was a realisation that membership was necessary in order that the islands could defend their interests at GATT in the future. By late May, Dominica, St. Lucia, and St. Vincent had become GATT Contracting Parties, although Grenada was not to become a member until February 1994. However, the applications of Dominica, St. Lucia, and St. Vincent had not been processed when the GATT Panel ruled against the EC's existing banana regime on 19th May 1993, a decision ratified by GATT's governing council on 16th June.

The panel recommended that the EC remove the discriminatory quota arrangements that were maintained by the UK, France, Spain, Portugal and Italy. In addition the panel found that the EC preferential tariff for ACP banana exporters violated Article I (most-favoured nation treatment), in that the benefits of the EC's banana policy were restricted to a small group of countries. The panel asked the EC to bring its tariff rates for Latin American banana producing states into line with those for other GATT members (GATT Panel Report, DS32/R). Although the GATT Panel only ruled against the national banana regimes and not the new single market regime, the ruling was significant as it set a precedent for the future. By ruling against the national regimes, the Panel opened up the possibility of a successful challenge against the new regime, which came in February 1994. The second Panel argued that the common regime violated the principle of most favoured nation treatment, and that the distribution of licences was unfair (GATT Panel Report, DS38/R).

Even though the EU was able to prevent adoption of the GATT report by voting against rulings that required unanimity for acceptance, the EU was keen to minimise the international opposition to its banana regime, while also wanting to increase the regime's wider credibility. As a consequence the EU signed a compromise 'Framework Agreement' with four of the five Latin American complainants, which involved increasing the quota for dollar bananas, lowering the associated tariff, and allocating a majority of the dollar quota to the four Latin American signatories. In return the Latin Americans undertook not to initiate dispute settlement procedures against the EU's banana regime for the duration of the agreement (European Commission, 1994).

Despite the fact that the Framework Agreement was designed to end legal challenges to the EU's banana regime in the GATT, the reaction of the ACP was not entirely favourable. The additional banana volumes entering the EU as a result of the agreement led to an increase in market supply pressures, and precipitated a decline in prices which adversely affected the returns for ACP banana growers. Further, the provision within the Framework Agreement for a quota of 90,000 tonnes for non-traditional ACP exports also proved controversial. The ACP had agreed a formula for allocating this tonnage fairly equally between non-traditional suppliers and traditional suppliers of non-traditional quantities in both Africa and the Caribbean. However when the actual allocation was made the European Commission acted without reference to the ACP, and gave the bulk of the quota to the Dominican Republic and Belize. The decision created an amount of bad feeling between the Caribbean and African producers in the ACP group, as the African nations felt that the Caribbean had benefited at their expense. Both Cameroon and the Ivory Coast felt that the Commission had not properly considered the likely increase in their future banana production, and with no additional quota their capacity to expand was constrained. Perhaps, more importantly, the quota issue distracted the ACP from the wider challenges that were building against the EU's banana regime at that time.

The Increasing Interest of the United States in the Banana Dispute

During the summer and autumn of 1994, the United States government began to take an increasing interest in the banana issue, precipitated by the growing feeling on the part of some US companies that the EU's regime, together with the newly agreed Framework Agreement, seriously discriminated against them. The first indication of more serious opposition to the EU's regime came in September, when Chiquita and the Hawaii Banana Producers Association called on the United States Trade Representative (USTR) to act. The USTR responded by launching an investigation under the unfair trade provisions of Section 301 of the US Trade Act. Section 301 allows the USTR to take action (including unilateral measures) against policies of foreign countries that harm US commerce. During the months that followed, the USTR in the guise of Mickey Kantor increased the pressure on the EU to make its banana regime more acceptable, albeit with little success (PrNewswire, 1994 and Caribbean Insight, June 1995). As a consequence, in August 1995 the USTR indicated that attempts would be made to resolve the dispute at the World Trade Organisation (WTO), the more powerful successor to the GATT, supported by a new Section 301 investigation.

The US Administration, although pushing ahead with the WTO complaint attempted to reassure the Caribbean banana producers that they did not want preferential access to end in the EU, rather to overturn a regime that was unfair to its corporate interests. However the Caribbean banana producing countries were not reassured, despite high-level discussions with the US. The US was unyielding in its opposition to certain aspects of the EU's banana regime, which exasperated the Caribbean representatives who accused the US of not being prepared to negotiate and having already made up its mind to refer the dispute to the WTO. The Caribbean's mood was not improved, when both Costa Rica and Colombia were threatened with trade sanctions if they refused to withdraw from the Framework Agreement. Indeed, Costa Rica and Colombia only managed to avoid sanctions by agreeing to address US exporters' complaints and to cooperate with the US in its opposition to the EU's banana regime.

The motivation for US involvement in the banana issue has been questioned, as it is unusual for the USTR's thinly staffed office to devote resources to a case in which few US jobs are at stake, particularly when only around a dozen cases a year are accepted by the USTR, and even fewer are taken to the WTO. Only a very small amount of bananas are produced in the US, all of which are grown in Hawaii, and even though Chiquita is a significant US concern, most of its 40,000 workers are based in Honduras and Guatemala. Suggestions have been made that financial donations from Carl Lindner, a staunch Republican, and his American Financial Corporation, the parent company of Chiquita, to both Democrats and Republicans had been important in persuading the US to take action against the EU's banana regime. It seems that Chiquita was anxious to regain market share lost since the EU's banana regime was introduced, while also attempting to make up for losses sustained in the Far East and Eastern Europe. Carl Lindner has declined to comment on the alleged link between political donations and government action, while the US government itself has argued that such events are nothing more than coincidence.

The First WTO Panel: A Marginalization of Caribbean Interests

The first moves to challenge the EU's banana regime at the WTO were taken in September 1995, when the US filed a petition at the WTO supported by Guatemala, Honduras and Mexico. This first petition was then dropped when Ecuador, the world's largest banana exporter, entered the WTO and sought to join the dispute against the EU's regime. A second petition was then filed in February 1996, which superseded the first and now included Ecuador as one of the complainants. After unsuccessful consultations were undertaken between the parties to the dispute (the US, the EU and the four Latin American countries), the complainants asked for the creation of a dispute panel, a request that the Dispute Settlement Body (DSB) acceded to on 8th May.

The Panel consisted of Kym Anderson, Director of the Centre for International Economic Studies in Australia, Christian Haberli, executive director of the GATT/WTO division of the Swiss Ministry of Economic Affairs, and Stuart Harbinson, permanent representative of Hong Kong to GATT/WTO, and the Chairman of the Panel. The Caribbean and other ACP banana producing countries were extremely disappointed with the composition of the panel, believing that none of its members truly represented the interests of developing countries in the dispute. Of more significance however, was the fact that the ACP countries were only allowed third party rights at the panel hearings, which meant that they were grouped together with countries such as Canada, India, Japan, and Thailand, who had no direct interest in the dispute (WT/DS27/R/ECU). However within the context of the WTO third party status meant that the ACP countries were, for the first time, excluded from direct involvement in a process which was considering the future status of their banana exports. Further, the WTO had the power to demand changes to the EU's banana regime, irrespective of the views held by the ACP. In the past the banana producing interests of the ACP were able to directly access the policy process both at the national and European levels, in order to make sure their interests were secured.

At the Panel hearings in September and October both the EU and the ACP states, the latter doing so under their third party status, set out a legal defence for the provisions of the EU's banana regime, while the complainants, along with Paraguay, presented arguments against the regime. There was a perception on the part of the Caribbean that during the hearings the Panel was receptive to those arguments that suggested the EU's regime was a restriction on free trade, while dismissing submissions which argued that the regime was an important mechanism in promoting economic development. In addition the legal defence set out by the Caribbean was blunted somewhat by the fact that only permanent government employees were allowed to sit in on Panel hearings. As a consequence a number of advisers to the Caribbean banana producing countries, including those with legal experience, were barred from the Panel hearings after the US delegation protested at their presence. Three officials were excluded who had been accredited by St. Lucia, but were informally representing 12 countries in the ACP group, while a lawyer representing St. Vincent, a former deputy USTR, was also ejected. Only Ambassador Edwin Laurent of the Eastern Caribbean Mission was allowed to remain. Small states such as St. Lucia and St. Vincent were unable to employ the necessary expertise on a permanent basis and had legal advisers when required. The ejection of these advisers from the Panel hearings angered Ambassador Laurent, who subsequently argued, 'Small countries like mine have no power ... All that is on offer is rough justice' (Caribbean Insight, 20 April 1997). The exclusion of a number of accredited representatives of the small Caribbean states exacerbated the feeling that the nature of the WTO discriminated against the particular needs and circumstances of the smaller contracting parties of the organisation. The perception that the WTO was insensitive to the needs of small less-developed states grew during the time which the EU's banana regime was being considered at the WTO.

The publication of the WTO's final ruling came in May 1997, which upheld several elements of the complaint lodged by the US and the four Latin American countries. The Panel did rule that the EU could continue to give preferential access for traditional ACP bananas, a change from the GATT Panel rulings, which had themselves precipitated the EU to organise a waiver to exempt the Lomé Convention, and therefore its banana regime, from GATT's most favoured nation commitment. Nevertheless, the Panel recommended 'that the Dispute Settlement Body request the European Communities to bring its import regime for bananas into conformity with its obligations under GATT, the Licensing Agreement and the GATS' (WT/DS27/R/ECU). An unsuccessful appeal was heard by the Appellate Body in July and in September, two weeks after the Appellate Body report was released, the DSB adopted the ruling. Under WTO rules of negative consensus, which meant that a ruling could only be blocked if the benefiting party voted to reject the favourable Panel decision, the EU and the ACP were unable to prevent adoption of the report, a very important difference from the previous GATT dispute settlement rules. The new system thus shifted the balance of the dispute settlement process away from the defendant and towards the complainant, which meant changes to the EU's banana regime that were stipulated by the WTO had to be implemented. The EU, therefore, undertook to reform its banana regime to meet the WTO ruling and was given until 1st January 1999 to do so, much to the annoyance of the US who thought it too long a period for compliance.

The rulings of the Panel and the Appellate Body, meanwhile, were strongly criticised by Caribbean politicians and officials. For example, the then Prime Minister of Dominica, Edison James, argued, 'We feel betrayed by the WTO, because we joined the Organisation believing that its primary purpose was to bring about improved living standards and equity and fairness in international trade'. While Ambassador Laurent claimed, 'The experience of the case has exposed blatant shortcomings in the (WTO disputes) system. These must be addressed in any reform, including the necessity to take into account the impact of decisions especially when, as in this case, the affected countries have vulnerable and fragile economies. It is already too late for our bananas case, maybe the right improvements can yet be made to a system which would be helpful to the participation of small developing countries and reassure them that the system is not structurally weighted against them' (The Courier, No. 166, 1997, p. 60). From the Caribbean perspective the banana case at the WTO illustrated the narrow remit of the organisation in terms of the development/liberal trade dichotomy, and the risk of marginalization of small states at the WTO. Although there is some merit to these arguments the former issue has to be qualified, as the WTO did not rule against preferential access per se, but just the nature of the system which sustained that access. It could be argued that in reality the principle of preferential access, and the way in which that access was safeguarded, were so closely linked that the ruling against the latter negated the former, but it was hoped that reforms to the regime would be possible which would secure the position of Caribbean bananas in the European market.

However, it is important to recognise that the ruling by the WTO was a seminal moment in re-defining the Caribbean's role in shaping the nature of the EU's banana trade. There was now an actor which had the power to override the traditional interests of the Caribbean which had been so central in both the UK, and latterly the EU banana trades during the twentieth century. The Caribbean had no choice but to accept the Panel ruling and to prepare for the changes that were necessary to make the banana regime WTO-compatible. Further, the governmental nature of the WTO meant that those interests that represented the Caribbean banana growers and associated companies were excluded from this higher level of arbitration and were therefore obliged to continue their lobbying efforts at the national and regional level, in order to make sure that their interests were not neglected at the WTO. Nevertheless the context of the dispute should be recognised in that the effect the WTO had on ACP interests is partially due to the nature of the banana issue, in that the dispute was primarily between the US and the EU, which meant that the ACP only had third party status. As a consequence the ACP were marginalized in the dispute settlement process, which meant that they were grouped together with countries who had no direct stake in the issue under consideration. The WTO process did not discriminate against the interests of the ACP states per se, but rather the particular nature of the issue under adjudication meant that the ACP's influence was constrained.

Reform and Resistance: New EU Proposals and a Second WTO Panel

As with the negotiations for the design of the EU's original single market regime in the late 1980s and early 1990s, the method of policy formulation was similar, although the dynamics of the process were different. Unlike in 1992 when a new regime had to be designed from scratch, the changes needed in 1998 were less fundamental. In addition, the Commission was more experienced in handling the banana portfolio, with the regular contacts within the Banana Management Committee proving most useful in judging what kind of changes would be acceptable to Member States. As a consequence the actual discussions for a revised regime were less controversial than those for the original regime and agreement was reached between the Member States in June 1998 (Council of the European Union General Secretariat, 1998). The compromise entailed the abolition of the import license system which discriminated between ACP and dollar operators and the retention of a revised quota system designed to sustain duty-free access for ACP banana producers. The Commission and the Presidency were both pleased with the changes, believing that the banana reforms would make the regime WTO compliant, while also honouring the EU's commitments to the ACP banana producers under the Lomé Convention. The new banana regime came into force at the beginning of 1999 and was due to last at least until the end of 2004 (Official Journal of the European Communities, 1998a). However, as soon as the compromise proposal was agreed, those countries that had taken the EU's original regime to the WTO indicated that the revised proposals did not go far enough in meeting WTO compliance.

When unsuccessful attempts were made by the US to persuade the EU to make further changes to the revised regime, the USTR outlined plans at a meeting of the WTO's DSB in October for unilateral action to be taken under Section 301 of the Trade Act against the EU for alleged inaction to comply with the WTO ruling. Such action was condemned by the EU, as being illegal under WTO law. The EU argued that sanctions were only allowed when authorised by the DSB. Despite the stand-off between the EU and the US, Ecuador broke ranks with the US and the other Latin American complainants to begin the process of reconvening the WTO Panel that had considered the EU's original regime. Then, in an unprecedented move, the EU asked the DSB to set up a Panel to examine the EU's reformed regime. Usually it is the complainants who request the establishment of a Panel, but in this case the EU wanted to ensure that the dispute was arbitrated within the WTO in order to avoid the imposition of unilateral sanctions by the US.

The dispute worsened in late December when the USTR published a list of 16 products from the EU on which it was threatening to impose 100 per cent duties, covering trade to the value of US$520 million (Inside Europe, 21 December 1998). The US maintained that such action was permitted by the WTO because the EU had failed to amend its banana regime to be fully consistent with WTO rules and that the increase in tariffs would be equivalent to the harm caused by the EU regime. The US followed this course of action because they feared that the normal WTO process would take too long, thus restricting the USTR's ability to take action. Despite the hope that the WTO would effectively promote a new approach to global trade, the realities of diplomatic horse-trading transcended any high ideals that may have existed. The determination of the US to force the EU to design a regime which met its requirements risked usurping the role of the WTO as the final arbiter in international trade disputes.

At the heart of the dispute between the EU and the US was an interpretation over two articles of the Dispute Settlement Understanding. The EU believed that in the circumstances Article 21.5 should take precedence, in that any doubt over the compatibility of the revised regime should be decided through recourse to the dispute settlement procedures. The US meanwhile believed that it had a right to impose sanctions under Article 22, which allows a member of the WTO to ask for authorisation to suspend trade concessions when a third party has not implemented WTO findings. The US were concerned that if Article 21.5 took precedence, implementing measures could be continually changed if challenged, with no recourse to Article 22 and the right to receive compensation or to suspend trade concessions. The problem was that this was the first case in which compliance had been disputed and it took the WTO into uncharted legal waters. WTO rules permit retaliation, but they were ambiguous about how compliance should be determined. Therefore there was no authoritative rules laying out the relationship between Articles 21.5 and 22 of the Dispute Settlement Understanding.

Despite the threat of sanctions the DSB established the Panels requested by Ecuador and the EU on 12th January 1999 and were due to complete their work in April, although this was at least a month after US sanctions were scheduled to be applied. As a consequence, the US prepared to ask the DSB on 25th January to approve its trade sanctions. However, when the US attempted to get WTO approval Dominica and St. Lucia, supported by the Ivory Coast, effectively delayed the examination of the US request for authorisation of sanctions by blocking the adoption of the agenda, the first time this had happened. Under WTO consensus rules, meetings cannot proceed if the agenda is not accepted. The representatives of Dominica and St. Lucia argued that it was illogical for the WTO to consider the US request at a time when a Panel had just been established to rule on WTO conformity of the EU's revised banana regime. In an associated press release it was argued

> that the Dispute Settlement Body cannot be seen to undermine the dispute settlement process, which lies at the very foundation of the multilateral system. As founding members of the WTO, the islands were concerned that a dangerous precedent might be set, if the US was permitted to act on a unilateral determination as to whether the EU's regime is WTO compatible (Embassies of the Eastern Caribbean States and Mission to the European Communities, 26 January 1999).

Although blocking the DSB agenda was only a temporary expedient and had no direct bearing on the final outcome of the banana issue, it was an important gesture on the part of two small states highlighting the fact that their rights and interests had not been fully recognised during the time which the WTO had considered the banana issue. As regards the banana dispute itself, such action on the part of Dominica and St. Lucia can be seen as a last act of defiance before the US and Latin American complainants finally got their way. Nevertheless, the US was deeply critical of the move and accused the EU of colluding with the two Caribbean states, an accusation strongly denied by the EU and the islands. With the agenda blocked the meeting was adjourned to allow the WTO director-general to find a compromise to break the deadlock.

A compromise plan was agreed between the EU and the US on 29th January which postponed the unilateral imposition of US sanctions against EU products until 12th March at the earliest. In return the Panel created to consider the validity of the EU's revised banana regime would also examine the US request for sanctions and to set the value of any penalty. Despite the fact that the threat of sanctions had been postponed, some EU Member States were concerned about the wider ramifications of the dispute. Italy in particular, strongly criticised the effect it was having on the wider trading environment, a view supported by a number of European companies whose products were at risk from US sanctions. There was a belief in some quarters that the EU's commitment to safeguard preferential access for ACP bananas was damaging European economic interests and as a result there was a realisation that defending the banana regime was becoming more trouble than it was worth.

There was an expectation that on 2nd March the WTO Panel would report on the amount of sanctions that the US could apply on EU goods, with Washington planning to ask the WTO's dispute settlement body the following day to authorise sanctions based on the recommendations of the Panel. However the arbitrators gave the US and EU only an initial report on how they intended to proceed and requested additional information from both sides. In response the USTR announced that the US Customs Service would begin 'withholding liquidation' on imports valued at US$520 million on selected products from the EU. In a move that the EU maintained broke WTO rules, US customs on 3rd March ordered importers of the products on the sanctions list to post bonds of 100 per cent of the goods' value, although the US would refrain from collecting higher duties until the release of the arbitrators' final decision. The US used the bond mechanism to ensure that the delay in the WTO arbitrators' decision did not result in delaying its timetable for the unilateral imposition of sanctions.

The final decision from the WTO Panel came in April 1999, which found that the EU's revised banana regime was still inconsistent with WTO rules in a number of respects, while at the same time authorising the imposition of US sanctions, which the Arbitrators agreed should be implemented up to a total of $191.4 million, i.e. just over a third of the amount the US was originally claiming (WT/DS27/ARB and WT/DS27/RW/EEC). On the 9th April the office of the USTR published a revised list of European products which would be subject to a suspension of concessions and on 19th April the WTO Dispute Settlement Body authorised the action. It is ironic that after the second WTO panel the immediate result was not a liberalisation of the EU's banana regime, but an increase in trade protectionism on the part of the US to punish the EU for its perceived intransigence, a move authorised by the WTO itself. The operation of the WTO's dispute settlement system proved to be more complicated, both politically and technically, than was the expectation when the WTO was established, highlighting the fact that even a legally based trading organisation was not above domestic political considerations. However, despite the complicated, and at times controversial events that surrounded the second WTO Panel, it is important to remember that the interests of the ACP banana producers were once more under threat. After the first WTO Panel the ACP banana interests had been able to use its network of influence at the national and European levels to secure a revised EU regime which sustained their preferential access. However, once the banana issue returned to the WTO the ACP interests were again marginalized as a result of the nature of the new dispute settlement system.

It can be argued that with the development of the WTO as a new arena of decision-making to challenge the role of the EU, the Caribbean banana interests became less engaged with the policy process. Within the context of the EU the ACP interests were able to influence the decision-making process directly, as the actors were considered to be legitimate by politicians and civil servants and were consulted regularly. However, within the context of the WTO the ACP banana interests became detached from the main arenas of influence, being relegated to third party status, with no direct role in the process. The ACP interests were unable to gain proper recognition at the WTO due to the nature of the issue under consideration. Both status and strategy were pre-determined within the framework of WTO rules and so there was little opportunity for the ACP states to adopt a particular strategy to improve their standing within the dispute settlement process. The ACP interests became marginal players within the WTO not through choice, but through design. Therefore as the banana dispute moved between the European and international levels of decision-making, the banana interests of the ACP oscillated between having an active interest on the one hand and being marginalized on the other. The more distant the decision-making process became the more damaging were the policy outcomes for the ACP.

The Politics of Fatigue: A Final Settlement?

There was a feeling of inevitability when the WTO Panel gave its judgement. On 21st April, the EU decided not to appeal against the ruling, and undertook to amend the regime. With no appeal forthcoming the Panel Report was adopted by the DSB in early May. The European Commission then set about the task of reforming the EU's banana regime once more.

However the divisions between the various actors with an interest in the banana issue remained, both regarding the options for reform and whether the options on offer would be compatible with WTO rules. Despite these deep differences of opinion the European Commission, after extensive consultations, finally adopted a proposal to revise the EU's banana regime at the beginning of November 1999. The proposal was based on two stages. The first stage entailed introducing a transitional tariff rate quota system, which would maintain both the current GATT bound quota and the autonomous quota. The preferred option for the distribution of licenses was a system based on a historical reference period, although if this proved unacceptable a 'first come first served system' could be introduced. In addition a new third quota would be open to all suppliers, although ACP bananas would be accorded a 275 euro/tonne preference. The distribution of this quota would be undertaken by auction. After a period of transition a tariff only system would enter into force in January 2006, with the ACP receiving an appropriate tariff-preference (European Commission, 1999).

However, once again the intractability of the banana dispute meant little progress was made in reaching an agreement. After eight months of intensive discussion between the European Commission and the WTO complainants, the auctioning system was rejected as it was not favoured by any of the major parties to the dispute who could not decide on the reference period for licences. As a consequence, in early July 2000 the Commission proposed that 'It will continue to study a transitional system of tariff quotas, but at this stage on a "first come, first served basis" for the three tariff quotas'. The Commission also asked the Council of Ministers to provide it with the authority to begin negotiations under Article 28 of the GATT (to establish a new tariff level) with the relevant suppliers, 'in order to implement a flat tariff system, in case no solution can be found on the tariff quota basis' (European Commission, 2000). In early October the General Affairs Council accepted the Commission's proposals for reform, despite strong opposition from the European Parliament who believed the provisions would not safeguard vulnerable ACP producers (Caribbean Insight, 13th October 2000, Commission of the European Communites, 2000, and European Parliament, 2000).

The patience of the European Commission and Council was now waring thin. The pressures within the EU were growing for any kind of resolution to be found, as the wider economic interests of the Union were being further damaged. For example two European firms sought compensation from the EU for alleged damages as a result of the banana dispute between the EU and US. In addition, Ecuador received the support of the WTO's Dispute Settlement Body to apply sanctions worth $201.6

million on trade with the EU because of the banana regime, while the US threatened to impose further sanctions on EU goods, if a settlement was not found, through the 'carousel' system whereby sanctions on goods are rotated over time.

The Caribbean's position through this period of negotiation was to reiterate the importance of the banana export trade to a number of its islands economies. In addition the Caribbean argued in the strongest terms possible that both the 'first come, first served system' which would have ended guaranteed access for its bananas into the EU market, and the tariff-only regime were unacceptable. However, the banana interests in both the Caribbean and more widely in the ACP saw their position being marginalized in the negotiations, for a number of reasons. Firstly, the French and Spanish producers who had been allies of the ACP lobbied for the 'first come, first served' system, thus undermining the united front that had existed between the EU and ACP banana producers in the past. Secondly, a number of the WTO complainants indicated that in the absence of an agreement on bananas they would block the EU's request for a WTO waiver for the newly agreed Partnership Arrangement (Cotonou) between the EU and the ACP, the successor to the Lomé Convention. The WTO complainants hoped that by threatening such action the unity of the ACP would fragment between those that produced bananas and those that did not, and that the greater prize of the Partnership Arrangement would make both the EU and the ACP more willing to come to an agreement over bananas. The final and most important issue was that the EU was obliged to undertake discussions with the WTO complainants, and the US in particular, to make sure that any changes to the regime were acceptable to them. This was necessary in order to prevent any further action at the WTO being taken and to end the US sanctions on certain EU imports which were in place. The need to find a solution to the dispute thus outweighed the concerns the ACP had regarding whether the outcome of the negotiations would adequately safeguard their market access.

Indeed, the pressure exerted by the US and Chiquita finally paid off at the beginning of April 2001. After almost 16 months of discussion it was revealed that the EU and the US had reached a settlement regarding the banana dispute. Under the agreement the EU consented that the distribution of licences would be based on historical trading patterns, rather than the 'first come, first served' system suggesed by the Commission in July 2000. In addition, the Commission reduced the import quota for ACP bananas by 100,000 tonnes to 750,000 tonnes, while the autonomous quota favouring dollar bananas increased from 353,000 tonnes to 453,000 tonnes. The third quota category, also primarily for dollar bananas, remained at 2.2 million tonnes. The EU further committed itself to move to a tariff-only system in 2006. In return, the US removed its $191 million of sanctions, imposed on the EU in April 1999, and agreed to support the EU's attempt to obtain a WTO waiver to allow for the continuation of the exclusive ACP quota until 2006 (Office of the United States Trade Representative Press Release, 11th April 2001). The new import rules took effect at the beginning of July 2001. The EU's Agriculture Commissioner Franz Fischler showed his relief that an agreement had been found when he stated 'the decision shows the determination of the Commission to end this never ending story. We are delivering' (Caribbean Insight, 4th May 2001).

The agreement particularly benefits Chiquita, who will gain most from the quota changes; an indication of this became apparent when the company's share price rose by 50 per cent on the news of the settlement (Financial Times, 12th April 2001). Dole and the independent banana producing country of Ecuador were originally unhappy with the compromise, as both had been in favour of a settlement which would have discounted past performance. Indeed, earlier in the negotiating process Ecuador's ambassador to the EU complained that the EU and Ecuador had been 'virtually taken hostage' by the US government (Caribbean Insight, 13th October 2000). However, after reassurances from the Commission regarding technical aspects of the new regime, Ecuador swung behind the agreement. As for the Caribbean producers, even though they will be guaranteed sales above current levels in the agreement, the medium-term future looks bleak. The EU has been forced to favour those interests that have opposed the regime at the WTO at the expense of the ACP, in order to secure an end to the dispute which has damaged the wider trading interests of the EU. With the solution to the banana dispute being a tariff only arrangement for the EU market, it is questionable whether such a system will be able to meet the obligations in the new Banana Protocol attached to the Partnership Agreement between the ACP States and the EU which commits the latter 'to examine and where necessary take measures aimed at ensuring the continued viability of the ACP banana export industries and continuing outlets for ACP bananas on the Community market' (Horne, 2000).

Conclusion

It can be argued that the ACP/EC, and particularly the Commonwealth Caribbean banana interests, were highly effective in their lobbying efforts within the Community. The advantage of being familiar with the European institutions allowed those interests that wanted preferential access to be sustained in the new regime, to gain a strategic advantage over the 'liberal' banana interests. In addition the role played by a number of Member States and the European Commission in defending the ACP/EC position was highly significant. However, due to the complex, fragmentary and open nature of the European policy process, as compared to the close institutional links that had underpinned the ACP interests at the national level, the safeguards achieved for traditional ACP banana suppliers were less than before. The single market was much larger and more fluid in its construction than the UK market, which meant that the traditional suppliers had less protection against market instability. Further, the institutional mechanisms that had helped stabilise the UK market, particularly the Banana Advisory Committee, were replaced by a European wide Banana Management Committee made up of civil servants from each Member State, and chaired by the Commission. Contacts still existed at the national level, but they were less important than in the past.

However even though the Caribbean/ACP were able to safeguard their interests prior to the creation of the single market in bananas, the period after the single market's enactment saw a series of challenges against the EU's banana regime which fundamentally undermined their position. The creation of the WTO Dispute Settlement Process meant that the Commonwealth Caribbean became only peripheral players in defending a regime for which they had so successfully lobbied. Rather the EU was obligated to meet the legal requirements stipulated under WTO law. The institutional nature of the present international trading environment superseded national and regional commitments to retain a long term trading relationship. The Commonwealth Caribbean lobbying effort continued at the national and regional level, but there was now a new level of arbitration, in the form of the WTO, which marginalized their efforts. As the EU's banana regime was not theirs to defend, the Commonwealth Caribbean become third parties in a dispute between the two great trading areas of the world, the US and the EU. The increasing role of the US government, along with Chiquita Brands International, was also important in that the banana dispute took on a significance that bore little relation to its actual importance, with ramifications for the future operation of the WTO, the power of multinational companies, the place of small island states in a more integrated international economy, and the nature of the US-EU trading relationship. In short, the 1990s saw a significant marginalization of Commonwealth Caribbean banana interests, whereby the future of their banana exports to Europe is now in serious question.

References

ACP Secretariat (1991),Comparative analysis of the ACP and French positions on the common rules necessary for the management of the market for bananas in the Single European Market, June.

Benelux Economic Union (1990), Memorandum of the Governments of the Three Benelux Countries, Commission for Foreign Economic Relations, September.

Caribbean Banana Exporters' Association (1990), Joint response of the Caribbean Banana Exporters Association and their marketing partners to the United Kingdom Government proposals on common arrangements for bananas based on a European quota for dollar source imports, London, 2 May.

Caribbean Insight, incorporating the Caribbean and West Indies Chronicle, Caribbean Council for Europe, London.

Commission of the European Communities (CEC) (1992a), Setting up the internal market in the banana sector, Report compiled by a Commission ad hoc 'Bananas' Interdepartmental Working Party working to Commission guidelines, Commission working document, SEC (92) 940 final, Brussels, 12 May.

Commission of the European Communities (CEC) (1992b), Proposal for a Council Regulation (EEC) on the common organisation of the market in bananas, COM(92) 359 final, Brussels, 7 August.

Commission of the European Communities (CEC) (1995), Report on the Operation of the Banana Regime [SEC (95) 1565 final: 11/10/95], Brussels.

Commission of the European Communities (CEC) (2000), Communication from the Commission to the Council on the 'First Come, First Served' method for the banana regime and the implications of a 'tariff-only' system, COM (2000) 621 final, Brussels.

Council of the European Union General Secretariat (1999), 2110th Council Meeting, Agriculture, 9558/98 (Presse 214), Brussels, 26 June.

The Courier, Journal of ACP and EU Affairs, Commission of the European Communities.

Embassies of the Eastern Caribbean States and Missions to the European Communities (1999), Windward Islands object to sanctions request in WTO, Press Release, 26 January.

Eurolink newsletter, Organisation of Eastern Caribbean States Joint Mission in Brussels.

Europe/Caribbean Confidential, Caribbean Council for Europe, London.

European Commission (1994), Commission Announces Resolution of Banana Dispute with Latin American Countries, IP/94/265, 29 March, EC Spokesman's Service, Brussels.

European Commission (1996), Commission Proposes Modifications to the Banana Regime, IP/96/206, 6 March, EC Spokesman's Service, Brussels.

European Commission (1999), Commission proposes to modify the EU's Banana Regime IP/99/828, 10 November, EC Spokesman's Service, Brussels.

European Commission (2000), Commission proposes solution to end banana dispute, 4 October, EC Spokesman's Service, Brussels.

European Parliament (2000), MEPs infuriated by Commission proposals for banana deal, News Report, 11 July, Brussels.

European Standing Committee A (1992), European Document No. 8372/92, Relating to the Common Market Organisation for Bananas, 9 December, HMSO, London.

General Agreement on Tariffs and Trade (1993), EEC-Member States' Import Regimes for Bananas, DS32/R, 19 May.

General Agreement on Tariffs and Trade (1994), EEC-Import Regime for Bananas, DS38/R, 11 February.

Horne, J. (2000), Address of the ACP President in Office the Hon. John Horne, Minister of Trade, Industry and Consumer Affairs of St. Vincent and the Grenadines on the occasion of the 30th Session of the ACP-EU Joint Assembly, Abuja, Nigeria, 20-23 March.

Inside Europe, Caribbean Council for Europe newsletter, London.

Official Journal of the European Communities (1989), Resolution on ACP bananas, The ACP-EEC Joint Assembly, C186/46-47, 24 July.

Official Journal of the European Communities (1992), Resolution on ACP bananas, The ACP-EEC Joint Assembly, C211/55/5 and 60/1, 17 August.

Official Journal of the European Communities (1993a), Commission Decisions (92) 3381 and 3382 of 28 December 1992, C1/4, 5 January.

Official Journal of the European Communities (1993b), Opinion of the Economic and Social Committee on the Commission Regulation (EEC) on the common organisation of the market in bananas, C19, 25 January.

Official Journal of the European Communities (1993c), Legislative Resolution embodying the opinion of the European Parliament on the Commission proposal for a Council regulation on the common organisation of the market in bananas, C21, 25 January.

Official Journal of the European Communities (1993d), Council Regulation (EEC) No. 404/93 of 13 February 1993 on the common organisation of the market in bananas, L47/1, 25 February.

Official Journal of the European Communities (1993e), Commission Regulation (EEC) No. 1442/93 of 10 June 1993, laying down detailed rules for the application of the arrangements for importing bananas into the Community, L142/6, 12 June.

Official Journal of the European Communities (1993f), Action brought on 14 May 1993 by the Federal Republic of Germany against the Council of the European Communities (Case C-280/93), C173/17, 24 June.

Official Journal of the European Communities (1993g), Order of the Court of 29 June 1993, (Case C-280/93) R Federal Republic of Germany v. Council of the European Communities, C199/13, 23 July.

Official Journal of the European Communities (1998a), Council Regulation No.1637/98 of 20 July 1998 amending Regulation (EEC) No. 404/93 on the common organisation of the market in bananas, L 210/28, 28 July.

Official Journal of the European Communities (1998b), Council Regulation (EC) No. 2362/98 of 28 October laying down the detailed rules for the implementation of Council Regulation (EEC) No. 404/93 regarding imports of bananas into the Community, L293/31, 31 October.

Ramsaran, R. (1990), Negotiating the Lomé IV Convention, Institute of International Relations, University of the West Indies, July.

Roche, J. (1998), *The international banana trade*, Woodhead Publishing Limited, Cambridge.

Sandiford, W. (1998), The Proposed Amendments to the European Banana Regime: Would the Windward Islands be no worse off? OECS Secretariat, St. Lucia, October.

Select Committee on International Development (1998), The Renegotiation of the Lomé Convention, Fourth Report, 2 Volumes, Report and Proceedings of the Committee and Minutes of Evidence and Appendices, HMSO, London.

Stevens, C. (2000), Trade with Developing Countries: Banana Skins and Turf Wars, pp. 401-426, in H. Wallace and W. Wallace (eds), *Policy Making in the European Union*, Oxford University Press, Oxford.

Sutton, P. (1997), The banana regime of the European Union, the Caribbean, and Latin America, *Journal of International Studies and World Affairs*, Volume 39, Number 2, Summer.

World Trade Organisation (1997), European Communities - Regime for the Importation, Sale and Distribution of Bananas, Complaint by Ecuador, Report of the Panel, WT/DS27/R/ECU, 22 May.

World Trade Organisation (1997), European Communities - Regime for the Importation, Sale and Distribution of Bananas, Request for Consultations by Panama, WT/DS105/1, 24 October.

World Trade Organisation (1999a), European Communities - Regime for the Importation, Sale and Distribution of Bananas - Recourse to Arbitration by the European Communities under Article 22.6 of the DSU, Decision by the Arbitrators, WT/DS27/ARB, 9 April.

World Trade Organisation (1999b), European Communities - Regime for the Importation, Sale and Distribution of Bananas - Recourse to Article 21.5 by Ecuador, Report of the Panel, WT/DS27/RW/ECU, 12 April.

World Trade Organisation (1999c), European Communities - Regime for the Importation, Sale and Distribution of Bananas - Recourse to Article 21.5 by the European Communities, Report of the Panel, WT/DS27/RW/EEC, 12 April 1999.

World Trade Organisation (1999d), United States and Sections 301-310 of theTrade Act of 1974, WT/DS152/R, 22 December.

5 The Sugar Protocol

ANNA DICKSON AND TIDINGS NDHLOVU

Introduction

On 1st February 1975, at its very inception, the EC/ACP Sugar Protocol reaffirmed the significance of sugar in international trade agreements. The Sugar Protocol was the outcome of a lengthy debate on the formulation of new sugar arrangements for the EC to incorporate its new applicants for membership and British stipulations and conditions for entry. The Sugar Protocol is a continuation and extension of the Commonwealth Sugar Agreement (CSA) under which Britain imported a significant percentage of her domestic sugar requirements from the Commonwealth.

The Sugar Protocol provides the African, Caribbean and Pacific (ACP) sugar exporting states with their most important market in terms of quantities exported and prices obtained. There is a guaranteed market for 1.3 million tonnes of sugar annually at prices linked to those paid to EC farmers. The Sugar Protocol thus insulates the ACP against the worst vagaries of the international sugar market. In this respect, the Protocol is an exception to the Common Agricultural Policy (CAP), negotiated in the face of strong opposition from farming lobbies in the EC.

The Protocol is in fact a unique arrangement between developing and industrial nations because sugar cane is the only agricultural commodity produced in less developed countries (LDCs) which competes directly with a commodity (sugar beet) widely produced in more developed countries (MDCs). In 1974 the European Parliament noted that 'the question of sugar carries considerable importance in the eyes of the producer countries, since the solution reached will provide an example for other primary products which are crucial in the economy of the associate countries' (EP, 1974).

Nevertheless, the historical significance of the Sugar Protocol in British foreign policy and in the EC has been declining almost since its inception in 1975, but with much greater effect since the 1980s. There are a number of possible explanations for this decline which are explored in this chapter. One theme is that, when what was initially a British policy was handed over to the EC, this immediately meant that the special importance attached to Commonwealth sugar imports by Britain was diluted amidst the multiple sugar producing interests of the Member States.

Moreover, since the 1980s, it is arguable that there has been an ideological shift within the EC which, combined with the radical geopolitical changes resulting from the ending of the Cold War, have meant that historical commitments between the EC and the ACP are under threat. There is now a clear contradiction between the desire to meet historical obligations to the ACP and a public commitment to economic liberalism *à la* WTO. Furthermore, the interests of the member states have changed with each subsequent enlargement, and this means that the concerns of the ACP are not at the top of the external relations agenda, while the arguments for historical obligation which pertained to only a small number Member States have weakened. Consequently, when Lomé IV ended in February 2000, a radically new WTO compatible trade agenda was proposed for the Cotonou Agreement, including the ending of preferential trade access for all but the poorest ACP states. This excludes all Caribbean states (except for Haiti) which are middle income countries but, nevertheless, remain commodity dependent. The Sugar Protocol will cease to offer any comparative advantage to the ACP states after 2009, although it is clear, when looking at its operation throughout the period under review, that the value of the Protocol has been gradually eroded.

This chapter first traces back the historical origins of the conflicting interests in the world sugar market. This is followed by the role of institutional factors in the resolution of emerging conflicts. It is against this background that we examine the extent to which coagulating positions were played out in the CSA as a prelude to the Sugar Protocol. The Sugar Protocol was the outcome of a lengthy debate, over many years, on how best to protect Commonwealth sugar producers once Britain joined the EC. The seemingly unreconcilable interests were resolved by the onset of a world sugar crisis.

The operation of the Protocol is the subject of the fourth section of the chapter and demonstrates that there still remain many unreconcilable interests between ACP sugar producing states and the operation of the CAP. These have become more pronounced as the CAP is subject to external challenges from third parties through the GATT and the WTO.

The post-Lomé period is characterised by a radical departure from the original challenge to the principles of reciprocity and MFN embodied in Lomé, and the end of what was once a unique and much lauded Convention, toward the gradual adoption of trade liberalisation for all but the poorest as part of a wider commitment to economic liberalisation in line with WTO obligations. This also means that policies, such as the CAP and its sugar regime, will become increasingly difficult to justify to third parties and, indeed, to the WTO dispute settlement body. The Sugar Protocol comes under attack on both counts.

The Origins of the Conflict

It is in order that we tease out factors which may be regarded as having triggered the ensuing conflicts during the development of the sugar industry. First, the ending of slavery and emancipation was a long drawn-out affair (1883 to final abolition in 1888/89) and slavery exposed sugar producing colonies, particularly in the Caribbean, to new difficulties of rising cost of production, which threatened the very survival of the colonial sugar economy (see Albert, 1976, 1984; Albert and Graves, 1984, p. 3; 1988, pp. 2-3; Delson, 1984; Gonzalez, 1984; Price and Taylor, 1996, p. 14; and Schnakenbourg, 1984).

In addition, growing population and rising real wages in Europe and the USA, which increased demand for sugar, also opened up new opportunities which were taken up by the heavily subsidised and protected European beet sugar industry (see Albert and Graves, 1984, p. 1; 1988, pp. 1-2; Chalmin, 1984, pp. 9-11; Pigman, 1997, p. 192; Price and Taylor, 1996, p. 14; Richardson, 1984). By 1914, many developed nations had come to regard sugar as essential rather than a luxury. With the installation of more efficient production, transport and distribution methods, some cane growers followed the European example, while much of the Caribbean, the Philippines, Latin America and parts of Africa were slow to adapt (Chalmin, 1984, p. 19).

Clearly, the differential response to growing sugar consumption, particularly British consumption, and a changing duty structure, was dependent on the availability of external finance (and its associated indebtedness) and the ability to withstand precipitous falls in world sugar prices. Thus, the sugar industries were unevenly developed (see Albert, 1976; Albert and Graves, 1988, pp. 2, 13-14; Beechert, 1988; Nagano, 1988; Perkins, 1988; Pollitt, 1988; and Szmrecsanyi, 1988).

Over and above this, those planters who survived the restructuring of the industry clamoured for protection against the rigours of international competition. Attempts to return to free trade were prevented by the outbreak of the First World War and the ensuing economic crises. Crucially, international payments crisis threatened, which demanded the stabilisation of sugar export prices and the adoption of import substitution policies (ISP) 'to save foreign exchange'.

Finally, although from 1870 successive British governments espoused the principle of free trade, the policy was inconsistent and shaped by economic, political and cultural factors. A negotiated liberal trade regime in the international sugar market could benefit planters and refiners in Britain's sugar producing colonies, particularly the West Indian sugar industry. In addition, the interests of consumers of sugar had also to be taken into consideration: the abandonment of sugar subsidies would give them the cheapest possible sugar. On the other hand, if efforts for a 'negotiated' agreement failed, Britain's market power would ensure that a unilateral 'free trade' policy was in place, even though this had been ineffective from 1860 (Mahler, 1984, p. 712; Pigman, 1997, pp. 188-89, 191-209).

Ultimately, the British imperialists won the debate over free traders and the Brussels Convention was signed on 5th March 1902 (see Chalmin, 1984, p. 18; Guy, 1984; and Pigman, 1997, p. 205). Chalmin points out that:

> In many respects the Brussels Convention was a turning point. The renunciation of the system of bonuses was general and provoked a slight price increase, the first for half a century, cane sugar recovered on the export markets and the relative share of cane in world sugar production started to increase (Chalmin, 1984, p. 18).

Moreover, as shown below, there were times when international sugar market conditions conspired with the changing domestic political situation in Britain to push sugar prices higher (Pigman, 1997, pp. 201-02). At one point, to the consternation of British West Indian interests, the British government seemed under pressure from domestic consumers and sugar-using industries to be considered for withdrawal from the convention (Pigman, 1997, pp. 200-204).

Essentially, between 1902 and the outbreak of World War I, exposure to free markets was limited; and there was no reason why sugar export prices should be exposed to the cold wind of market forces. This situation is even more evident with regard to the more contemporary period. Table 5.1 and Figure 5.1 show that the only periods when prices tended towards convergence were between 1962 and 1963, 1964 and between 1970 and 1971. As demonstrated below, these were periods when there was little or no agreement in the international price of sugar in the world market.

Table 5.1 CSA and World Market Sugar Prices, 1960-1974

Year	CSA Negotiated Price[a] £ per long ton	World Free Market Price (London Daily Price)[b] £ per long ton
1960	44.44[c]	28.48
1961	45.10[d]	25.68
1962	45.76[d]	25.59
1963	46.04[d]	71.70
1964	46.04[e]	51.13
1965	42.00	21.51
1966	43.50	17.87[f]
1967	43.50	19.36[f]
1968	43.50	21.83[f]
1969	43.50	33.83[f]
1970	43.50	40.06[f]
1971	43.50	46.18[f]
1972	50.00	72.63[f]
1973	50.00	99.46[f]
1974[g]	61.00	-
1974[h]	140.00	305.13[f]

a. From 1950 to 1964, prices were bagged sugar, basis 96° pol. c.i.f. UK based on pre-war freight and insurance rates; from 1965 it was on a f.o.b. and stowed in bulk basis.

b. LDP which commenced in April 1956; and these are annual averages, basis 96° pol. c.i.f. free out, UK in bulk.

c. Settled at 1959 price review.

d. Negotiated by formula.

e. Price held (1963 review postponed).

f. From 1st January 1966 the basis of the LDP was altered from shipment in bags with cost of discharge for seller's account to shipment in bulk, free out i.e. with cost discharge for buyer's account.

g. To September 1974.

h. Remainder to completion of NP quotas.

Sources: International Sugar Yearbooks (for various years): Harris (1973, p. 12).

Figure 5.1 CSA and World Market Sugar Prices 1960-1974

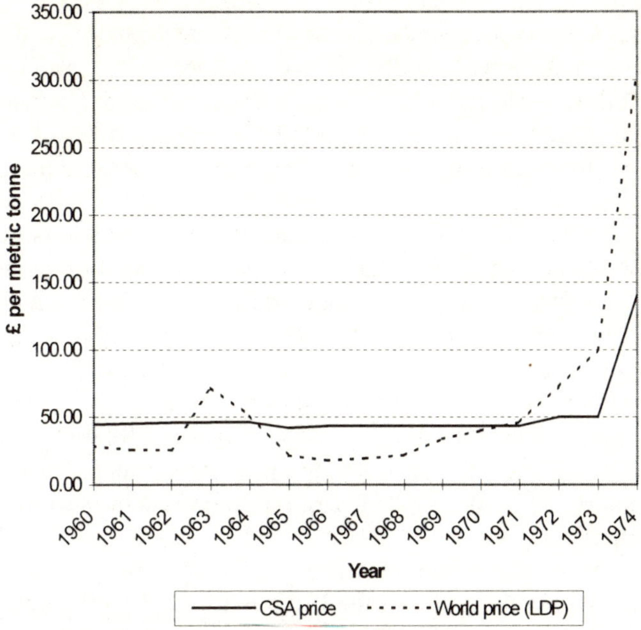

Stabilising The World's 'Free' Market?

It is important to establish to what extent efforts to 'manipulate' prices at the domestic and international level were successful in resolving the conflicts. In other words, how significant were agreements between countries in stabilising sugar prices? In addressing these questions, consideration is also given to the circumstances, which necessitated the creation of these international agreements.

To the extent that the First World War interrupted the Brussels Agreement by destroying European beet fields, then Britain's formal withdrawal in 1913 was no more than academic. Britain had remained the only major free market country supplying both the world and European markets, while the USA was a major importer. The Brussels Agreement was not, however, finally declared to have expired until 1920.

Meanwhile, the sugar shortage, consequent on World War I, resulted in a sharp rise in sugar prices. This meant that Cuba, which had become the world's largest sugar exporter, doubled its production in a bid to fill the shortage. To illustrate the volatility of the world market, fears of a bad harvest in Cuba after the war only fuelled speculative activities which, in turn, led to rising prices in an already booming market. This period of economic boom in Cuba was popularly known as the 'Dance of the Millions' (see Albert and Graves, 1988, pp. 5-6; Mahler, 1984, p. 713; O'Connor, 1970; Pollitt, 1988, pp. 97-99; Post, 1978, p. 43; and Thomas, 1971, p. 540). The uncertainty about output prices prompted states to intervene to manage production, thus price-setting practices became more prominent.

Britain, in particular, abandoned its free market policy. This led to a massive contraction of the world 'free' market - only 25 per cent of sugar produced was traded in the world market in the late 1920s, a figure which fell to 10% in the 1940s (Albert and Graves, 1988, p. 7). In a bid to attain self-sufficiency in sugar after the experience of shortages during the First World War, the British government instituted wartime tariffs and an excise tax rebate to encourage a nascent beet industry. This was followed by subsidies as in the case of European countries (see Albert and Graves, 1988, p. 5; and Harris, 1973, pp. 15-16). Britain embarked on securing guaranteed sugar suppliers.

From 1919 onwards, colonial preferences restricted imports only to those cane producers within the ambit of the British Empire. Significantly, accompanying measures to raise duties on sugar imports effectively excluded European beet producers, whose exports were almost always refined sugar, from the British market. Domestic political exigencies required that the British sugar beet industry be saved from ruin, since many of the factories were strategically sited in areas of high unemployment, rather than those areas where they could take advantage of agglomeration economies. Amalgamation (to form the British Sugar Corporation (BSC) in 1937) was the price the factories had to pay for such guarantees. Besides: 'An agreement was also reached between the BSC [now British Sugar PLC] and the British cane-sugar refiners, splitting the market between them. In return for the refiners' agreement to this arrangement, ... the British Government continued the tariff protection given to the refiners in 1928 against imports of refined sugar' (Harris, 1973, p. 16; see also Price and Taylor, 1996, p. 14).

The establishment of the International Society of Sugar Cane Technologists also signalled that technological exclusivity had few advantages in a world which was increasingly characterised by technically and politically determined markets and prices. Bilateral and multilateral deals became more commonplace, with the market playing an increasingly peripheral role (Albert and Graves, 1988, p. 15; Boomgaard, 1988, pp. 165-67; North-Coombes, 1988, p. 194).

Although being the biggest importer of Cuban sugar, the USA for its part, had always had protection as a central plank of her economic policy; from June 1930, America increased the duty on Cuban raw sugar, purportedly to give American producers a breathing space. Protests from US interests in Cuba prompted the USA to replace tariff barriers with quotas for US and foreign producers (see Huberman and Sweezy, 1960; O'Connor, 1970, pp. 5-29; and Pollitt, 1988b, p. 99). The ensuing 1931 Chadbourne Plan, or 'Gentleman's Agreement' as it was known, failed to control supplies to the US market. While Cuba kept to the spirit of the agreement by reducing production, her partners, and those consuming countries which were not party to the agreement, increased their production (see Mahler, 1984, p. 714; and Pollitt, 1988, pp. 100-4). The resulting low prices prompted further attempts to cut production, restrict protectionism, and stabilise world sugar market prices in the shape of the 1937 International Sugar Agreement (ISA) (see Smith, 1973, p. 59). This Agreement included 21 signatories from different countries who together accounted for about 90 per cent of world production. Fixed quotas for both traded and domestically consumed sugar were agreed upon. Producers were thus anxious to come to some agreed 'remunerative' price for sugar; buffer stock schemes, even if their record of operation was still patchy, seemed to be one way of stabilising sugar prices.

However, the 1937 ISA was undermined by interruption to production occasioned by World War II. Once again the USA and the UK resorted to bulk-buying in order to safeguard their supplies. Once war ended, the British government, indebted to the Commonwealth for its role in the war, continued to favour supplies from the Dominions (e.g. Queensland in Australia) and colonies, culminating in the 1948 'purchase guarantee for all their exportable sugar, at prices to be negotiated annually, which later in 1951, laid the basis for the longer-term arrangements under the...CSA' (Price and Taylor, 1996, pp. 14-15; see also Abbott, 1989, pp. 343, 345; Southgate, 1984). Because of shortages caused by post-war dislocations in the European agricultural sector and the Korean War, market prices skyrocketed.

From then onwards, ISAs were negotiated in response to fluctuating free market prices. Quotas were often used to adjust/maintain prices within the desired range. There was to be a minimum and maximum price objective. The assumption was that prices could be fixed so that crises of shortages and overproduction could be managed. From 1951, economic 'provisions' (some would say, penalties) were added to the agreements.

These have been in force except for the years 1962-68, 1973-77 and 1985-88.

The political background should also be taken into account when considering the extent to which ISAs stabilised world sugar prices. For example, following the Cuban revolution in 1959, international management of sugar prices suffered a severe blow as relations between Cuba and the USA deteriorated. By 1960, relations had worsened to the point that the USA cut Cuban sugar quotas to zero. These quotas were reallocated to over 24 countries. Cuba looked to the USSR and other Eastern European countries which, for the period 1965-70, bought Cuban sugar at prices 'well above ruling world market prices and very roughly in line with prices paid by the USA and the CSA negotiated price' (Cutajar and Franks, 1967, p. 62). Since the USSR and Eastern European countries were already self-sufficient in beet sugar, they disposed of any surplus onto the 'residual' world market, depressing world market prices.

It is, however, fair to say that, apart from the period 1988-1998 (see below), the period 1952-1960 was one of comparative stability, thanks to the effectiveness of the 1953 and 1958 ISAs in stabilising prices (see also Figure 5.2). Nevertheless, in 1961 the attempt to renew the 1958 ISA was foiled by Cuba's demand for a 10 million ton increase in its production by 1970 (see Roca, 1976; and Mahler, 1984). The effect was a free-for-all, followed by a rapid rise in prices in 1963, and a sharp fall in the mid-1960s.

Let us look at some examples of ISAs which were either effective or unsuccessful in stabilising world sugar prices. The Agreement made for the period 1968-73 was successful only insofar as it lasted in text the full five years and was associated with the raising of low and unstable prices which had been characteristic of the intervening period (see Figure 5.2; also see Smith, 1973, p. 59). Like the 1953 and 1958 agreements, the 1968 agreement was based on negotiated maximum exports which were set as a proportion of basic export tonnages (BETs). These BETs were intended to reflect the participants' desire for increasing their export earnings and maintaining prices which were 'reasonably remunerative' to producers (hence the minimum and maximum range).

Against the background of the USA's refusal to participate in the negotiations of the 1968-73 ISA because of Cuba's inclusion in the negotiations, and the EU's refusal to participate in the negotiations until such time as its proposed production quotas were revised, the ISA seemed unable to stem the surging prices after 1971. As producers increased their production in order to reap high profits, they could not be drawn into fresh negotiations. By late 1973, world market sugar prices had accelerated dramatically due to the shortage of sugar which had resulted from poor harvests (of 1973-74) in Cuba, the USSR (which had, by this time, become the mainstay of the free market), and Western Europe. In response, governments gave producers incentives such as subsidies to increase production

By contrast, the 1977 Agreement was generally ineffectual for several reasons. Firstly, there was basic oversupply in the world market, together with high stocks. Secondly, the USA, which was the largest importing member and seemed to be more interested in maintaining its market share (to satisfy the soft drinks industry) than the price it paid for raw sugar, did not ratify the agreement until 1980. In the 1970s, the US, Japan, Canada and other high income countries 'accounted for more than two thirds of the import market' (Hannah, 1998, p. 9). Thirdly, Cuba sought a larger share of the free market, particularly against the background of the USSR's planning for self-sufficiency in sugar. Lastly, the EC refused to join the ISA though it participated in the International Sugar Organisation (ISO). The principle of 'quotas based on past or current performance' was unacceptable to the EC at a time when its expansion programme was under way. With increasing scepticism over the reliability of the ISA's reports on special stocks (due to a lack of tight monitoring) and its inefficacy in stabilising prices (due to failure in releasing stocks at the appropriate time), the ISA's activities began to be seen as contributing to speculation in the shrinking world sugar market (see FAO, 1985).

Figure 5.2 ISA Price Agreement and World Sugar Prices (ISA Daily Prices)[a] 1958-1997

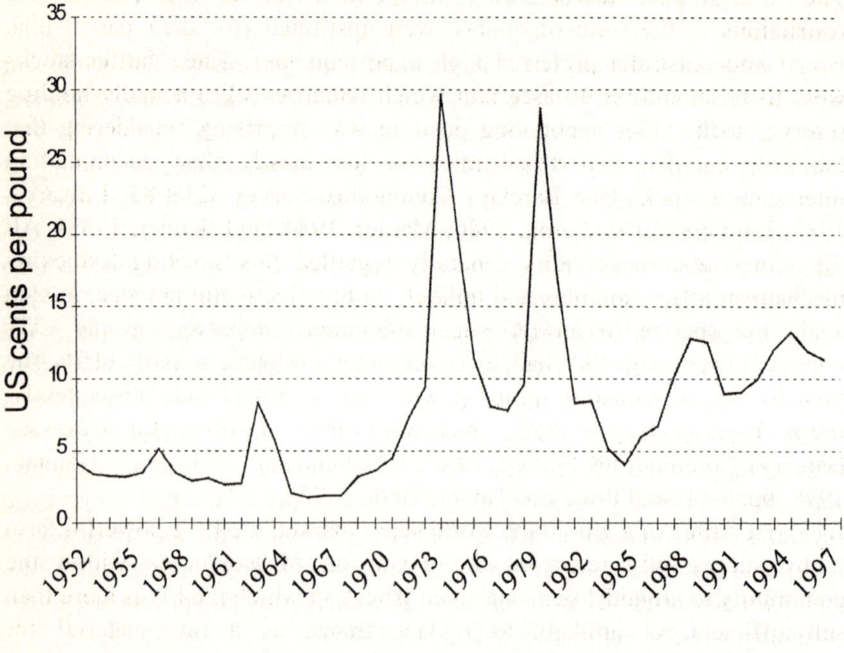

a. The international Sugar Agreement/Council Daily price is arrived at by calculating the arithmetical average of the London Daily Price and the New York Spot Price for that day after conversion of both these prices to US cents per pound, *avoidupois* f.o.b. and stowed Caribbean Port, in bulk, or if the difference between these two f.o.b. prices is more than 6 points, by adding 3 points to the lower of the two prices. 1960-1962: New York No. 4 (World) contract (f.a.s. Cuban port basis). 1997-1998: f.o.b. and stowed Far East Port, in bulk.

Sources: FAO 1978: 21; 1979: 23; 1985: 12; 1986: 30. International Sugar Yearbooks (for various years); Harris (1974: 12); T. Hannah, Head, Economics and Statistics Division, ISO (correspondence 26.02.98; 27.02.98: 14.07.98).

In an environment of high stocks and low prices, ISA members were desperate to see the EC participating in a new agreement. This was the background against which the 1983/84 negotiations took place in the ISO. The EC argued that it would only join the ISA if buffer stocks, rather than restrictions in the form of quotas, were instituted (for their part, Cuba, Brazil and Australia preferred high export quotas). These buffer stocks were to be monitored to ascertain which countries were actually holding reserve stocks. This negotiating position was surprising considering that the EC regarded export subsidies as less costly than accumulating intervention stocks (see Barclays Commodity Survey, 23/4/82; Edwards, 1983; Laidlow, 1983; Leroy, 1980; Mahler, 1984; and Stainer, 1983). All the same, other negotiators generally regarded this stocking/destocking mechanism as too complex and unlikely to be effective in practice, raising again the spectre of an EC sugar mountain. Moreover, so the EU's argument went, the ISA had to cover other sweeteners, particularly the high fructose corn/maize syrups (isoglucose or HFCs) and, subsequently, inulin fructose syrup in 1992, which were direct substitutes for sugar (see Barclays Commodities Survey, 24/6/83; Erlichman, 1983, p. 23; Hannah, 1998, pp. 9-11; and Price and Taylor, 1996, p. 25).

At a time of a glut in the world sugar market, the EU's powerful farm lobby successfully restricted the expansion of isoglucose within the community to around 1 per cent. Even wheat, in which the EU is more than self-sufficient, is unlikely to replace maize as a raw material for sweeteners, because 'the combined power of the sugar beet and sugar refining lobby would easily trounce any alliance between wheat growers and the fragmented food manufacturing industry in Europe' (Erlichman, 1983, p. 23). Indeed, in 1994, the EU decided to regulate inulin fructose syrup via quotas, and its production was finally subjected to the self-financing system (Price and Taylor, 1996, p. 25).

Finally, the major sticking point concerned market shares. There was no agreement on the allocation of Reference Export Availabilities (REAs) i.e. those representing 'normal' levels of exports of the ten big exporters. Without an agreement, the talks broke down in June 1984, and the principle of withholding stocks over and above REAs when prices were below a certain point was not put into practice.

Subsequently, the EC did join the ISA. With previous differences still unresolved, the 1985 ISA did not include economic provisions to stabilise prices. It operated solely as an administrative agreement on sharing information. After failing to thrash out points of disagreement, the ISA was extended in its administrative capacity for another year up to the end of 1987. For its part, the 1992 ISA Agreement also urged members to 'give due consideration to environmental aspects in all stages of sugar production' (article 30, UNCTAD, 1992, p. 18).

By 1996 the structure of the import market had changed. The oil price shocks of 1973 and 1980 contributed to the shift in the import trend: while high income developed countries had been responsible for two thirds of the import market in the 1970s, by 1996 the developing countries had increased their relative share to approximately 60 per cent of the market (Hannah, 1998, pp. 9-10). The extent to which this shift affected the stability of world sugar prices is considered below.

For the moment, we can note that agreements between countries began to be more significant in the determination of sugar prices. The 'residual' market had shrunk even further because of these agreements and bargaining. Nevertheless, free world market sugar prices have fluctuated from time to time despite international sugar agreements to stabilise them.

The Commonwealth Sugar Agreement

The Commonwealth Sugar Agreement (CSA) signed in December 1951 included the British Caribbean colonies, Fiji and Mauritius, Australia, South Africa, and the East African territories. The CSA committed Britain to purchase 1.64 million tons of sugar at an annually negotiated price, reasonably remunerative to efficient producers, for herself and New Zealand. The quota was later increased and redistributed to total 1.717 million tons (approximately 1.74 million long tons tel quel). For her own consumption, Britain would also import additional amounts of sugar under a preferential tariff. While quotas for the colonies exceeded those of the 1937 ISA by some 60 per cent, those of the Dominions rose by 30 per cent. The consequent expansion in the 1950s and 1960s was achieved 'at the expense of British beet producers, whose acreage was strictly controlled by the Ministry of Agriculture (although in the 1950s and early 1960s British beet was in fact uncompetitive with CSA cane-sugar, whose costs of production were considerably low)' (Ravenhill, 1985, p. 221). British beet producers were compensated for higher costs of production by a higher price than CSA exporters until (middle 1960s) they had increased their yields relative to Caribbean producers, at which point (1968) they received the same price (ibid, p. 222). The quotas were sufficiently flexible to give participants a rolling eight year guarantee which was considered a reasonable period for cane sugar producers, so the argument went, to plan expansion and continuity (see Abbott, 1989, p. 349; McDonald, 1996; Mahler, 1981, 1984; Moynagh, 1977; Prasad and Akram-Lodhi, 1988,

p. 44; Price and Taylor, 1996, p. 15; Southgate, 1984).

In addition to providing a price traditionally above the level of the world price, Britain also paid a special payment to the less developed exporting countries. This was calculated annually and ranged from about £7-£11 per long ton, depending on the world market price for sugar. Special arrangements were made for the Caribbean colonies to receive the maximum payment each year.

The CSA guaranteed price[1] was more stable from 1960 to 1972, with a sharp rise in 1973-74 (see Table 5.1 and Figure 5.1). Under the CSA, the guaranteed price was based on a cost of production index. Initially, price increases were determined by a formula based on a rather vague principle of paying a 'reasonably remunerative price' to 'efficient producers'. But from 1965 - a move subsequently reinforced by the 1971 price negotiation which introduced a two-price system; and influenced by the EC sugar price in the light of Britain's entry into the Common Market (as it was known) - the price fixing procedure took account of changes in production costs of Commonwealth countries (see Persaud, 1973, p. 88), so accommodating the high cost of production in the West Indies. Clearly, this suggests a cost-plus producer-led pricing system, not a consumer-led system. Thus consumers had a small role in the determination of sugar prices.

The CSA was important in encouraging the development and expansion of Caribbean sugar industries. It provided assured foreign exchange, employment, and facilitated higher wages and better standards of living. In the period from 1951 to 1961, total sugar exports from the Caribbean had risen from 1.5m long tons to 2.6m long tons. The Agreement lasted until 1974, making it one of the longest and most important Commonwealth agreements. During this period, the price offered to the producers was only below the world market price in eight out of the twenty four years (Ravenhill, 1985, p. 222). The CSA was, for the most part, a recognition by Britain of the dependence of the developing Commonwealth on the export of sugar and the effect on them of depressed world market prices (PRO, 1959).

For Britain, the CSA provided a reliable supply of raw sugar for refining, and for consumption needs not met by home production. The CSA ensured that Britain had the most reliable supplies of sugar in the industrialised world (see Abbott, 1989, p. 343; Castle, 1975; and Harris, 1973, p. 17). Although prices to British consumers were higher than world market prices, they were generally lower than sugar prices in most Western industrial economies.

When Britain first applied to join the EC in 1961, it was with cautious hesitation and an unwillingness to threaten Britain's traditional relationships with the USA and the Commonwealth. In 1959, the Chancellor of the Exchequer had stated what he considered to be the major difficulties in the way of UK entry to the EC: first of all, a Common Commercial Policy with the EC would fundamentally change trade relations with the Commonwealth and 'would in practice be damaging to the Commonwealth'. Secondly, the CAP would conflict with the Agriculture Act, and while British farmers could expect the same extent of protection under the CAP, the Commonwealth interest would not be safeguarded. A Common Import Policy would mean that the open market for Commonwealth food producers in the UK would disappear. Thirdly, Britain would not join the EC if it meant political unity. Finally, 'it cannot be assumed that the Six would be prepared to have us in on terms which would begin to safeguard the Commonwealth position' because it would mean that the UK market would not be open for the other members of the EC (PRO, 1959).

The issue of Commonwealth interests was clearly a major concern when Britain made the first unsuccessful application to join the EC. When Britain reapplied in 1967, sugar remained an important issue despite a recognition that Commonwealth exports were now stagnant and that the Commonwealth was in some ways a constraint on Britain's economic growth. Britain put forward the proviso that some agreement for her Commonwealth sugar producers, minus Australia, would be necessary if Britain entered the EC.

However Britain's entry was again vetoed, ensuring that the potential conflict was averted. From the deliberations on how to extend the guarantees to the CSA exporters without jeopardising British entry to the EC, an all party group of MPs who were opposed to the common market, and committed to the Commonwealth, emerged (Southgate, 1984). Thus the 1967/8 negotiation, though unsuccessful, had turned the future of Commonwealth sugar into a politically sensitive issue.

Meanwhile European beet farmers, in particular the more efficient French beet farmers, began to lobby for the right to supply the British sugar market if Britain became a member of the EC. They argued that Commonwealth sugar had outlets in the USA, and that British interests, led by Tate and Lyle, were only trying to defend the relics of the colonial system. The arguments were mostly directed at Tate and Lyle who were now buying their way into European beet, having reduced their commitments in the Caribbean. Pitted against 'important elements of the EC agricultural bureaucracy, heavily committed to the CAP, and politically important Community (especially French) beet interests'

(Mahler, 1981, p. 482) was an uneasy alliance of the sugar cane producers from ACPs, Tate & Lyle, the smaller Manbre & Garton [with 15% of the UK market for refined (cane) sugar], and the cane sugar refinery workers in the UK (see also Brown, 1972, pp. 138-39; Price and Taylor, 1996, p. 15).

In 1971, Geoffrey Rippon, then Minister of Agriculture in the Conservative government, conceded (to his potential EC partners) that only 1.4 million long tons of sugar from Commonwealth countries - at a price equivalent to that paid to beet producers in Europe - should be guaranteed entry after the expiry of the CSA in 1974. Indeed, the EC 'could not...offer more to the ACP planters of sugar cane than the European beet farmers without running serious political risks' (Schiffman, 1975, p. 5).

In discussing the conditions for British entry to the Community in 1971, it was decided that Britain should continue to import sugar under the current arrangements until the end of 1974 when the CSA expired, and that the African, Caribbean and Pacific states which were members of the CSA or the Yaounde Conventions would be offered a choice between association and a trade arrangement, and that sugar would be considered in this context.

There was no precedent for any such arrangement in the EC. In fact, prior to 1968 the French colonies of Madagascar and the Congo had guaranteed quotas in the French market, at prices on par with the price of sugar from metropolitan France and her DOMs. In 1968 the EC import levies had effectively excluded these sugar imports from the European market. Although France continued to import sugar for refining and re-export only, the quantities covered were very small. The Netherlands also had an agreement to import specific amounts of sugar from Surinam each year. These arrangements were terminated when the EC Commission ruled that they contravened the Community's sugar regulations (Lister, 1988).

That Commonwealth sugar should receive special treatment, other than under the normal terms of association, would be extremely difficult to negotiate and, even more so, to justify. Despite this fact, successive British governments consistently insisted that there would be room in the enlarged Community for Commonwealth sugar imports. It is little wonder that Britain's negotiations for entry into the EC caused anxiety over what would happen to preferential agreements between the UK and Commonwealth countries, particularly since sugar had profound political implications (see *The Courier*, 1984, p. 4; Dodoo and Kuster, 1977, p. 49; Edwards, 1983; Gruhn, 1976; Laidlaw, 1983, p. 1; Mahler, 1984, p. 725; The North London Haslemere Group, 1974, pp. 4-6; Patterson, as cited in

The Times, 16/1/75; Ramphal, 1983, p. 2; Schiffman, 1975, p. 5; and Whiteman, 1998, p. 31).

The case for continued support of Commonwealth sugar rested on three main arguments: firstly, the dependence of the states in question on sugar exports and, in particular, on the British market; and secondly, the contribution of the CSA to the rehabilitation and modernisation of Commonwealth sugar industries. Thirdly, it was also based on the effectiveness of the CSA in providing supplies in times of shortage and, given the instability of the world market, the need for security of supply and price. Up until 1973, Commonwealth cane supplied 70 per cent of the British market.

In the Treaty of Accession signed in January 1972, Protocol 17 allowed the import of Commonwealth sugar at a negotiated price until the end of the CSA, while Protocol 22 offered the developing countries of Africa, the Caribbean, and the Pacific (ACP) a choice between association and a trade agreement. Protocol 22 also repeated the assurances drafted in May 1971 in Brussels. Thus, when Edward Heath's Conservative government took Britain into the Community in 1973, his government made this level of guaranteed access to the EC a condition of its entry - the famous *aura à coeur* statement in Protocol 22 of the UK's Treaty of Accession to the EC.

However, when the Labour government under Harold Wilson reiterated the Conservative government's guarantees to Commonwealth producers in its renegotiation of entry exercise in 1974, major disagreements surfaced. The fact that the British government(s) appeared to regard the CAP 'as little more than politically motivated subsidisation of agricultural interests within the Community' (Mahler, 1981, p. 481) made this debate more acrimonious. The fact that the costs of agricultural export subsidies were unevenly spread between budget surplus and deficit countries, with British taxpayers and consumers paying a disproportionately large part of the bill, only further soured the atmosphere.

The ongoing debate was resolved, not by compromise, but by the onset of a sugar shortage resulting from production failures throughout the world. The shortage affected world and Community markets, and led to unprecedented price rises. In November 1974, the world market price of sugar rose to a record £680 per tonne.

The sugar crisis led to severe doubts within the Community about its ability to meet its domestic requirements in times of shortage as demand exceeded production. Import subsidies and export levies were introduced to meet the increased demand and the area under sugar beet production was increased by 19 per cent. However, because of poor yields immediately following the crisis, production remained below demand for the following two years, and the shortage of sugar in the EC continued.

Fortuitously for the ACP sugar cane producers, the buoyant world market prices finally persuaded EC beet sugar producers that, given the shortage (rather than the 'normal' chronic oversupply) of sugar, cane sugar need not be totally excluded: 'No longer did it seem so undesirable to secure sugar supplies by granting Commonwealth sugar producers long-term access to Community markets even at the Community's support price...[Moreover] a Community sugar surplus no longer represented a costly liability to be disposed of at a loss, but a desirable moneymaker, a rarity in an increasingly expensive and unpopular Common Agricultural Policy' (Mahler, 1981, pp. 482-83; also see Mahler, 1984, p. 7).

Indeed, the negotiations for a Sugar Protocol were completed with Commonwealth sugar producers hopeful that world sugar prices might remain well above the price offered by the EC. The 'new Convention… had apparently succeeded in breaching a fundamental principle of the CAP – that no access should be allowed for imports from third countries if Community supplies could reasonably meet domestic demands' (Ravenhill, 1985, p. 225). It was against this background that Commonwealth sugar producers finally accepted a total quota of 1.3 million tons as in the CSA (see Hoffmeyer, 1982, p. 4; Laidlaw, 1983, p. 1; Ravenhill, 1985, p. 225; McDonald, 1996; Price and Taylor, 1996; Whiteman, 1998, p. 31 amongst others). The EC itself undertook to contain or limit over-production to self-sufficiency via complex quota purchase systems; and also limit demand via high internal consumer prices which would be independent of 'free' market prices.

By January 1975 a downward trend had begun as consumption fell back to pre crisis levels. As a result, since 1975, EC production has been in excess of consumption requirements. 'So long as the burden of economic costs imposed by the sugar regime does not become insupportable, or too blatant in terms of excesses generated, EC policy makers will accept them as part of the overall burden represented by the CAP which is regarded as being necessary on social and regional grounds and as a vital ingredient in the process of European integration' (Harris, 1985, p. 2).[2]

As Community production grew, it became more difficult to restrict exports to the world market, and the EC emerged as the world's second largest sugar exporter in 1981. The emergence of the EC as a major beet producer and exporter has done much to change the nature of the world market (Harris, 1985). In particular, the production of surplus sugar, which is sold on the world market, contributes to depressed world market prices, thus adversely affecting other sugar exporters. It also contributes to the sentiment that the Community does not need to import cane sugar to fulfil its consumption requirements. Consequently ACP sugar can be seen as surplus, with no legitimate place in the Community market.

The Sugar Protocol

Despite the growing pressure, particularly from EC beet growers, to discontinue the EC-ACP partnership agreement, 'the special importance of trade in sugar is reflected not only in the existence of a separate Protocol for this commodity, but also by the extent to which it continues to influence the entire implementation of the Convention' (ACP, 1977).

The Sugar Protocol guarantees are set out in Article 213 (Chapter 2) of Title II of the Lomé IV Convention, while the implementing arrangements can be found in Protocol 3 of Lomé I and subsequently unchanged in Protocol 8 of Lomé IV. The essence of the Protocol is that the Community can import, at guaranteed prices, specific quantities of ACP cane sugar which the ACP states guarantee to deliver. The Sugar Protocol is thus a legally binding obligation to buy cane sugar from the ACP, and a legally enforceable undertaking by the ACP to deliver the sugar. Unlike the Lomé Convention itself, which was renegotiated at intervals, the Sugar Protocol was agreed for an indefinite period ('perpetual' or 'not specified', depending on one's interpretation). To add to the confusion, there is a clause which stipulates that the Protocol may be denounced, subject to a two years' notice from both parties, but this clause was arguably included for juridical security. Thus, the Protocol appears to exist separate from the Lomé Convention with a life of its own. Furthermore, the safeguard clause (set out in Articles 2 and 10, latterly article 177, of the Convention), which could allow the EC to plead disruption of its own sugar sector (under GATT regulations), cannot be applied as grounds for reducing access for the guaranteed quantities of preferential sugar set out in the Protocol.

There are three groups of countries which enjoy preferential treatment under the Protocol. These are the ACP countries, the Overseas Countries and Territories (OCTs) and India. The specified quotas are set out in Article 3 of the Protocol. The total in 1975 was 1,304,700 tonnes, including 25,000 tonnes for India, and small quantities (58,200 tonnes) for Belize, St. Kitts-Nevis-Anguilla and Suriname, which were then OCTs. The 13 ACP states were allocated quotas totalling 1,221,500 tonnes. Since 1975 there have been a number of adjustments to the original quota allocations (see Table 5.2). These have been the result either of supply shortfalls and the redistribution of the shortfall amongst the other signatories, or of allocations to new members of the Protocol. When Surinam, Belize, and St. Kitts-Nevis each became independent, they maintained the quotas they had been allocated as OCTs. Zimbabwe became a signatory to the Protocol in March 1982, and the Ivory Coast in July 1983. Kenya, Uganda, and Suriname at present have no quota due to earlier shortfalls. The Dominican Republic, a major sugar exporter, became an ACP member in 1990, but she gave an undertaking not to apply for a sugar quota under the Sugar Protocol.

In 1995, the EC and the ACP agreed on additional, variable quantities of raw sugar to be guaranteed to EC refiners. These quantities are determined annually in accordance with the EC's internal market conditions - the so-called 'Bilan' of the refiners' needs. Not only is the ACP required to comply with the EC's WTO commitments, but it was also agreed that this Special Preferential Sugar Agreement would initially last for six years, with effect from 1 July 1995 (McDonald, 1996; Price and Taylor, 1996, pp. 17-18; Prasad and Akram-Lodhi, 1998, p. 45).

These measures were designed to accommodate Finnish entry and the full accession of Portugal. While this additional quota does not benefit from the full ACP guaranteed price, it seems to have re-focused attention on the opportunity for increasing the quotas of ACP states which had been previously lost during Portugal's accession to the EC. At the time, Portugal was allowed to import only 75,000 tons from ACP supplies at the world price, for a limited period. Since some of these ACP countries already had long term arrangements with Portugal (at the world price), it was not clear how this new separate arrangement had substantially changed the existing situation for them.

The Protocol provides for the marketing of these quantities of sugar in the EC. While it is often presumed that meaningful 'negotiations' between the buyer (primarily Tate & Lyle) and seller (ACP countries) take place regarding the level of the guaranteed price, in practice the EC's internal considerations take precedent (Article 5 (4) of the Sugar Protocol) (hence why Routh, 1988, p. 1 describes ACPs as 'silent partners' in the price fixing exercise). Any amount within the agreed quantities which cannot be marketed in the Community, at a price equivalent to or in excess of the guaranteed price, will be purchased by the Community. The price level should take into account all relevant economic factors (including the state of the world sugar market, see also Table 5.3), and it applies to sugar, c.i.f. (carriage, insurance and freight costs). Unlike the CSA price which

Table 5.2 Lomé: The Sugar Protocol Quotas, 1975/6-1998/9

Quota-Receiving Country	Agreed Quotas (metric tons of white sugar) 1975/76	1978/79	1985/86	1989/90 - 1998/9
Barbados	49,300	49,300	50,049	50,312
Belize (formerly British Honduras)	39,400	39,400	40,104	40,349
Congo	10,000	4,957	10,000	10,186
Côte d'Ivoire (Ivory Coast)	—	—	10,000	10,186
Fiji	163,600	163,600	164,862	165,348
Guyana	157,700	157,700	158,935	159,410
India [a]	25,000	25,000	10,000	10,000
Jamaica	118,300	118,300	118,300	118,696
Kenya	5,000	93	5,000	—
Madagascar	10,000	10,000	10,573	10,760
Malawi	20,000	20,000	20,618	20,824
Mauritius	487,000	487,200	489,914	491,031
St Kitts and Nevis	14,800	14,800	15,394	15,591
Suriname	4,000	2,667	—	—
Swaziland	116,400	116,400	117,450	117,845
Tanzania	10,000	10,000	10,000	10,186
Trinidad & Tobago	69,000	69,000	43,500	43,751
Uganda	5,000	409	—	—
Zimbabwe (formerly S. Rhodesia) [b]	—	—	30,000	30,225
Total	1,304,700	1,288,826	1,304,700	1,304,700

a. India, which had been a member of the CSA, continued to receive the remainder of the allocation even though it was, and still is, not a member of the Lomé Convention. This was incorporated in the Joint Declaration of Intent, annexed to the Treaty of Brussels under Protocol 22.

b. Southern Rhodesia's 25,000 ton quota was suspended in 1965 because of UDI. In October 1980 these quota portions were restored after independence as Zimbabwe, to replace the unfilled quotas of other countries. This initially meant India forfeiting its entire 25,000 tons, even though the 1.3m mark had not been exceeded.

Sources: ACP London Sugar Group 1996, 1998; Aggra Europe's CAP Monitor (Appendix 7) 1989; Hoffmeyer, 1982, p. 96; Lomé I Dossier (Protocol 3); Lomé II Dossier (Protocol 7); Lomé III (Protocol 7); Moyes, 1987, p. 60; Official Journal of the European Communities.

was f.o.b., higher transport and storage costs for ACP sugar cane producers, particularly during oil crises, can result in a lower price than that of their beet sugar counterparts in the EC. Moreover, the exclusion of such a big player as Australia from the Agreement had an unintended outcome: rules regarding shortfalls were more stringent in the Sugar Protocol than CSA precisely because Australia had all along been relied upon to make up any shortfalls (Ravenhill, 1985, p. 228).

Prices received by the ACP (like those in the EC) have been higher than world market prices every year since 1974/75, except in 1980/81 when there was a temporary world market shortage and consequently a large price increase in the world market (see Table 5.4 and Figure 5.3).

Overall, the EC often reacted to the production deficits by according European and ACP producers high increases in the guaranteed or 'negotiated' price, only to be followed by modest price rises to attempt to remove accumulating and costly surpluses. The increase in the Community's gross exports from 1 million tons in 1970 to about 5 million tons in 1980/81 also had important implications for price determination. Surpluses were, and still are 'dumped' onto the world market at below average cost prices. Thus there are no EC sugar mountains as such. This dumping served to limit opposition to increasing beet sugar production in the EC for export (relative to other agricultural activities), primarily at the expense of non-ACP sugar exporters such as Brazil, Thailand and the Philippines; and even some other ACP Protocol producers such as Fiji and Zimbabwe. The latter, in particular, while being a recognised globally-efficient sugar producer (in terms of low costs of production) and having exportable surplus, is restricted by its relatively small quota under the Sugar Protocol (see Harris and Tangermann, 1993, p. 120; IDS, 1998; Koch, 1989; and McDonald, 1996, pp. 139,147; Julian Price, 9/9/98). Undoubtedly, the Sugar Protocol is still much more valuable than the premium over the world market price providing guaranteed income and foreign exchange which is of particular importance to the small export oriented Caribbean states. However in terms of the operation of the Protocol the ACP argue that firstly, no real negotiations take place and secondly, that all relevant economic factors are not taken into account.

Table 5.3 World Production, Consumption and Trade (Million Tons, Raw Value), 1960-1987

Calendar Year	Production	Consumption	Closing Stocks	Total Trade				World Free Market	
				Exports	Imports	Net Exports	Net Imports	Net Exports	Net Imports
1960	52.3	49.2	21.4	19.3	19.1			11.5	11.2
1961	54.8	53.2	21.3	22.4	22.0			12.0	11.8
1962	51.2	53.5	23.9	18.5	18.3			11.7	11.5
1963	51.8	54.3	20.9	16.9	16.6			11.7	11.5
1964	59.3	54.2	24.6	16.8	16.3	14.4	13.9	11.4	11.0
1965	63.8	58.0	28.2	18.6	18.1	15.6	15.1	12.2	11.8
1966	62.7	59.8	29.4	18.2	15.2	14.8	12.8	12.3	12.3
1967	65.0	61.6	31.4	20.2	19.6	17.1	16.6	13.8	13.1
1968	65.4	64.7	31.0	20.6	19.2	16.8	15.4	14.3	13.0
1969	68.1	66.8	32.3	18.6	18.8	15.3	15.5	13.0	13.3
1970	71.1	70.5	31.6	21.8	21.3	18.1	17.7	14.0	13.7
1971	72.0	72.5	30.6	21.0	20.6	17.4	17.0	14.5	14.3
1972	73.7	73.7	30.1	21.9	21.2	19.1	18.4	16.7	16.0
1973	75.8	76.3	29.3	22.5	22.4	19.5	19.5	16.5	16.6
1974	76.4	77.3	27.9	22.1	21.5	19.9	19.3	16.2	15.7
1975	78.8	74.4	32.1	20.6	20.5	18.5	18.4	13.4	13.5
1976	82.4	79.2	34.3	22.8	21.8	20.0	19.0	15.5	14.7
1977	90.4	82.6	39.6	28.5	26.9	25.5	23.9	20.8	19.4
1978	90.8	86.4	43.8	25.1	24.8	22.4	22.1	17.5	17.3
1979	89.3	90.3	41.9	26.0	25.1	23.4	22.5	18.3	17.7
1980	84.5	88.7	37.7	26.8	26.8	23.1	23.1	19.4	19.5
1981	92.8	89.9	39.6	29.1	28.2	25.2	24.3	20.6	19.8
1982	102.0	94.0	46.8	30.4	29.6	27.3	26.5	21.7	21.2
1983	97.0	93.8	48.8	29.0	27.7	25.3	24.1	20.6	19.6
1984	99.2	96.7	50.9	28.5	28.1	24.3	23.9	19.2	18.9
1985	98.4	97.9	50.2	27.8	26.6	24.2	23.0	19.0	18.2
1986	100.0	101.3	48.9	27.2	27.1	22.6	22.5	18.2	18.1
1987	103.5	105.7	46.3	28.4	27.7	23.4	22.7	18.6	17.9

Sources: FAO (1983: 3); Harris (1986, p. 4); Hagelberg (1987, p. 18); ISO Sugar Yearbooks (various years); Telephone Conversations Tony Hannah, January 1988 and 10 November, 1988 (correspondence 5.11.98).

Table 5.4 EC and World Market Sugar Prices, 1975/6-1997/98
(Raw sugar: basis 96° polarisation, c.i.f. UK ports)

Year	ACP Guarantee Price[a]	World Price (Average London Daily price)
(July/June)	£ per metric tonne	£ per metric tonne
1975/76	160.28[b]	171.90
1976/77	205.02	128.44
1977/78	216.49	103.38
1978/79	223.79	98.74
1979/80	211.72	191.27
1980/81	197.15	278.93
1981/82	221.23	158.65
1982/83	247.72	111.88
1983/84	255.90	134.53
1984/85	275.12	91.50
1985/86	287.97	101.20
1986/87	353.02	103.84
1987/88	346.87	117.97
1988/89	325.82	168.66
1989/90	335.37	198.05
1990/91	346.14	133.59
1991/92	352.58	134.66
1992/93	405.02	156.34
1993/94	405.23	180.68
1994/95	424.21[c]	213.19
1995/96	443.01[d]	200.33
1996/97	405.87	172.75
1997/98	364.68	158.76

a. The EC price represents the guaranteed price for ACP sugar, including MCA (Monetary Compensatory Amount) adjustments up to December 1992. MCAs were abolished with effect from 1 January 1993.

b. For the purpose of statistical comparisons, it is possibly preferable to disregard the calendar year 1975 since the UK paid a special (so-called) 'supplementary' price of £260 per long ton (£255.89 per tonne). This was paid above the Lomé guaranteed/normal minimum price. Thus, if the supplemental price is used, the ACP price obviously becomes £255.89 per tonne and the average 1975/76 ACP price becomes £211.64.

c. A new definition of Green ECU was operative from 1 January 1995. 523.7 ECU/tonne was paid from 1 January 1995 (having previously stood at 433.7 ECU/tonne in 1993/94 and 1 July 1994-31 January 1995).

d. A technical adjustment (due to agrimonetary factors) but resulting in an unchanged guaranteed price (523.7 ECU/tonne in 1995/96, and subsequent periods of 1996/97 and 1997/98).

Sources: ISO Sugar Yearbooks, Correspondence: Colin Campbell, Booker Sugar Co Ltd (27.6.86; 11.1.88; 21.11.88), Carl B. Greenidge, ACP Group (20.2.98), Tony Hannah, Economics and Statistics Division, ISO (26.2.98; 27.2.98; 14.7.98).

Figure 5.3 The EU and the World Market Sugar Prices 1975/6-1997/8

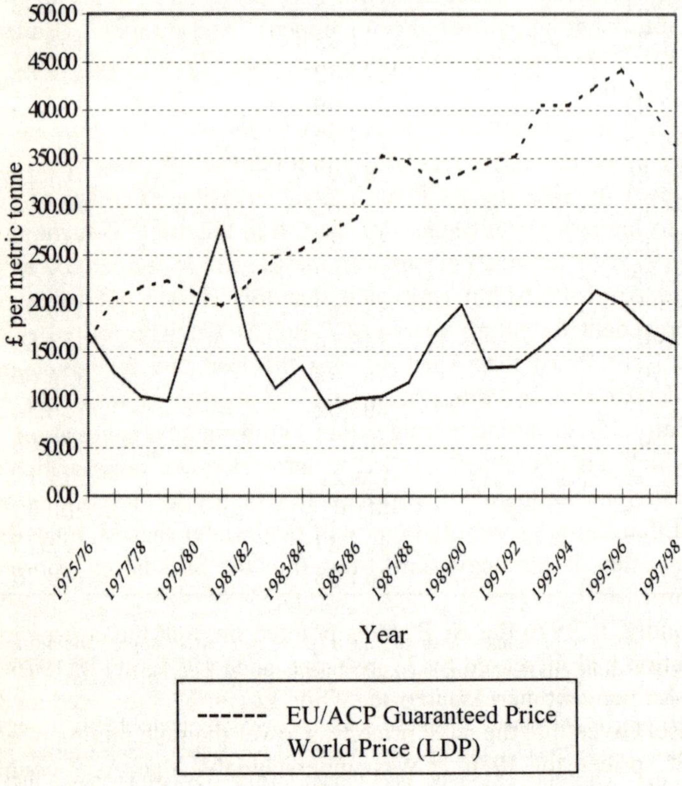

While ACP suppliers received much higher unit net returns at the beginning of the Lomé Agreement than during the CSA period, the failure of West Indian countries to fulfil their quotas proved to be short sighted. Meanwhile Mauritius and Swaziland received larger quotas than under the CSA. Mauritius, in particular, took the long view. Having judged that the sugar market could not continue at the high levels of 1974, the Mauritian government concluded that the best strategy for its sugar industry was price stability, which seemed to be on offer from the EC market. In contrast, the industries in Guyana and other Caribbean countries were under pressure from their governments to maximise short-term profits. In other words, while the sugar industries of the West Indies lobbied their governments for a stable price, the politicians just wanted 'money up front'. In Guyana, for example, the politicians allocated about 3 cargo-loads of sugar to Europe (in addition to what had already been shipped) - and no more! (Ravenhill, 1985, pp. 225, 228; personal correspondence with Julian Price, ED&F Man Sugar Ltd, 9/9/98).

The first price negotiations took place in June of 1976. From as early as this there emerged differences of opinion between the two parties as to the price level. Firstly, the ACP wished to have the price for that year backdated to January 1976, because of the fall in the price of sugar since it was set in 1975.[3] After much discussion, the EC finally agreed to backdate the price to April 1976, but cautioned that this should not be taken as setting a precedent for future years (ACP-EC, 1977). The formal rules of the Protocol stipulated that April 30 was the last date by which prices should be determined. In 1976, prices were not negotiated until 28th April, two days before the deadline, giving little room for actual negotiation. This practice, which has continued, has led to late price decisions, which then necessitate the backdating of sugar prices. In recent years it has been taken for granted that the price negotiations will begin later than stipulated and, in fact, they often do not begin until May, thus the backdating of prices is now the norm.

Secondly, in 1976 the ACP states pointed out that the cost of inputs into production had increased by 33 per cent since 1975. Yet in 1976 they received a 4.6 per cent increase in price while EC farmers received an 8 per cent increase. Given that the ACP price was lower than the minimum of the range of EC prices for 1976, it was understandable that ACP countries should object to their price being outside the range of prices in the Community. Subsequently the EC put forward a new method of calculating the ACP price, one which ensured that the revenue guaranteed to the ACP states was comparable to the net revenue of the producers of raw beet sugar in the EC (ACP-EC, 1977). The price finally agreed for 1976 proved to be a net decrease in income over 1975, but it was still higher than the cost of production even in the higher cost producer countries.

In 1981 there were further problems in the determination of prices when the new CAP sugar regime was formulated and the Commission offered a 7.5 per cent increase for raw sugar, and an 8.5 per cent increase for white sugar. The ACP reacted angrily to the price differential, which they believed was proposed to improve the profit margin of the cane refiners Tate and Lyle. A year later in January 1982, after much protest, the EC Council finally agreed to an 8.5 per cent increase in the price for raw sugar for the ACP producers (ACP-EC, 1981).

In 1983/84 dissent on price levels once again surfaced when the EC offered only a 4 per cent increase in price as part of an attempt to cut the cost of the sugar regime to the budget. By contrast, world prices (LDP) in the residual market were susceptible to relatively small changes in supply and demand, tumbling in the face of increased production which, in 1975-78, outstripped demand (see Table 5.3). World 'free' market prices fell to £165 per ton in March 1975. Whereas the average world price for the first five months (February/June 1975) in which the Sugar Protocol was in operation stood at £230.03 per ton compared with £147.59 for the average ACP guaranteed price, the world price collapsed in 1976 (see Table 5.4 and Figure 5.3).

By December 1979, a rumour about expectations of smaller crops in India, Brazil and Cuba than actually materialised set world prices rocketing to their highest level in three years. This trend had been fuelled by speculators (OPEC producers and investors) who moved from precious metals into sugar and other soft commodities in 1979 as a hedge against rising international price inflation and currency instability (see FAO, 1985). Regardless of the closing stock of 43.0 million tons in 1979 being more than adequate to cover the shortfalls in 1980 (see Table 5.3), and in spite of the subsequent release of special stocks, speculative activities guaranteed that world prices would continue to rise to the cyclical 'spike' of July/June 1980/81. By June 1985, the world price (LDP) had reached £68.40 per metric tonne which, using the Bank of England index of consumer price levels as the 'deflator', was the lowest in real terms since 1934[4] (see also FAO, 1986, p. 31). Here, prices were determined by a complex mix of factors: producer costs, speculation and geopolitics.

For its part, in 1985/86 the EC offered a smaller price increase for raw sugar than for white sugar for the second time. Once again the ACP protested at this decision. While their price had decreased in real terms, the refining margin for cane sugar had increased. Eventually, they were awarded a similar increase which 'represented an important concession of principle on the part of the EC authorities' (Czarnikow, 1986) and set a precedent for future years whereby the ACP could obtain the same price increase as EC white sugar producers.

In 1987 sugar prices were frozen. According to Colin Campbell, the freezing of the 1987/88 internal EC sugar price to the 1986/87 level was based on two considerations. Firstly, in order to fulfil its international 'responsibilities', the EC embarked on limiting sugar production within the Community as a way of reducing costly surpluses. Pressure came from GATT, UNCTAD, Australia (and other countries exposed in varying degrees to the free market) and the disciplines of the EC's own budget restraint. Secondly, there had been attempts to link all EC agricultural prices, even though there is still no formal system for this. The freezing of the internal price was partly in response to the concern that, if sugar prices continued to be high relative to cereal or dairy products, then farmers would move into sugar production, thus contributing to accumulating surpluses.

For many ACP economies, particularly given their own tendency to currency devaluation, fixed prices in ECUs are very valuable in terms of global purchasing power. This is even more crucial if one considers the declining influence of ACPs from the heady days of Lomé I when collective bargaining enabled them to extract some concessions from the EC, at one point even employing the ultimate threat of non-signature as a tactic (Whiteman, 1998, pp. 32-36). However, with the deteriorating economic conditions in the ACP states, particularly in Africa, the central role of the EC in the determination of the guaranteed price has become even more pronounced.

The EC price proposals for 1989/90 were made against the background of the Community agreeing in February 1989 'to take far reaching decisions on a multiannual programme of CAP reform for the late 1980s...The Community (has) embarked on a course aimed at imposing discipline on the agricultural budget of the EC and opening up CAP regimes to market forces' (MAFF, 1989). With reference to the sugar regime, the Community sought not only to open it up to market forces but also to continue to reduce the cost to the budget, to decrease the surplus and set an appropriate price level based on the prices of alternative arable crops and world market prices. The price for 1989/90 was cut by 2 per cent from July 1989. A new sugar regime in 2001 is likely to decrease the EU support price for sugar further.

The determination of prices by the EC in accordance with CAP guidelines means that all relevant ACP economic factors are not taken into account as stipulated in the Protocol. With respect to freight costs, for example, the guaranteed price for ACP sugar refers to unpacked sugar, c.i.f. European ports. This means that the ACP bear the transportation costs of the sugar from the ACP state to the EC port. In 1981, it was noted that freight charges had almost doubled in the previous two years and constituted a significant part of the cost of sugar production. The ACP wanted, not just a price increase, but, more importantly, a change in the basis of calculating the ACP price to include shipping. The problem is that any relief on freight charges would be considered as aid rather than trade. Both the ACP and the Commission have been trying to avoid the Protocol being treated as any form of aid. To date the policy remains unchanged.

The Post-Lomé Agreements

In relation to trade, the EU entered the post-Lomé negotiations with several objectives. Firstly, it was important to create an agreement which was more effective at promoting trade than the existing Lomé preferences had been. The general feeling in the Community was that the preferences had not been as successful as intended. ACP states have not fared as well as those states without similar levels of preferences.

Thus, the EU was keen to make any new trade agreement more effective at promoting trade and the integration of developing countries into the world economy. The Community views integration into the world economy as the chief means by which poverty and exclusion can begin to be alleviated. To this end, the economies of the developing countries should be made more liberal and the Community will assist in establishing the appropriate institutional framework to achieve this. Trade preferences, which are seen not to have worked, will be granted according to need, and phased out when that need is deemed to no longer exist (CEC, p. 1994).

This objective was constrained by the declared second condition, which was that all new or revised agreements and preferences must be made WTO compatible. The EU faces external manifestations of global liberalism, which support and justify this new orientation in development policy. The trend toward trade liberalisation which began in the mid 1980s gathered pace with the start of the Uruguay Round in 1986. The establishment of the WTO in 1995 reflected and reinforced this trend. This has resulted in a contradiction between the desire to meet obligations to the ACP and a commitment to economic liberalism. This contradiction was played out most vocally in the banana dispute between the EU and the US in the WTO but, in theory, could also be applied to the Sugar Protocol.

Lomé type preferences are said to be in breach of Article XXIV of the GATT which states that all trade agreements must be based on reciprocity. Any non-reciprocal trade agreements can exist only by the granting of a WTO waiver. Furthermore, special trade concessions for developing countries are permissible only if they are granted to all developing countries (again, unless there is a WTO waiver), according to Part IV of the GATT (otherwise known as the enabling clause of 1979). The Lomé Convention as a whole had a WTO waiver up till 2000. The EU and ACP must obtain a waiver to cover the transition period until the start of the new agreement(s).

Thirdly, the EU also claimed that it had no wish to dissolve a partnership of over twenty-five years, but such a relationship would nevertheless change in orientation. In particular, the EU has stated that there are limits to preferences in an environment of trade liberalisation.

The final Commission negotiating mandate stressed the importance of integration into the world economy. The assumption is that preferences are exceptions rather than the rule, and that the ACP must become competitive in the world market. Thus, the new Cotonou Agreement, which was signed by the ACPs and EU member states on 23 June 2000, provides for the setting up of new trade arrangements characterised by the 'progressive abolition of obstacles to trade between the parties in accordance with WTO rules' (The Courier, 2000, p. 5). The implications of this for the ACP are that only the least developed states, defined according to per capita income rather than any structural considerations, will be eligible for preferences. All other ACP states will enter into negotiations for new regionally based agreements in 2002, which will come into force in the year 2008 (Articles 29; 30; and 35.2).

It was also made clear by the EU that attaching the Sugar Protocol (Article 13) to Annex V of the New ACP/EU Partnership Agreement was in no way intended to degrade its status. If anything, this was just 'an institutional convenience'. Article 1 of the Sugar Protocol (concerning guaranteed prices, quantities and the indefinite nature of the Protocol) would still be emphasised. Indeed, while the Cotonou Agreement is for 20 years, with a clause stipulating that it be revised every 5 years, the Sugar Protocol would continue even after the Cotonou Agreement ceases to exist.

'The Council and the Commission will start by the year 2000 a process which by 2005 will allow duty free access for essentially all products from all LDCs building on the level of existing trade provisions of the Lomé Convention' (CEC, 1999). This process was subsequently followed by a Commission proposal for the EU to grant tariff-free and quota-free market access for 'everything but arms' (EBA) exported by LDCs (Liaison News, 2000, p. 19).

In extending the benefits of Lomé to all developing countries, the development policy of the EU becomes more WTO compatible. Nevertheless, it should be noted that most LDCs are already members of the ACP and, clearly, the so-called 'everything but arms' (EBA) proposal which was agreed by the EU foreign ministers on 26th February 2001 (by a qualified majority) only results in nine additional LDCs.

Against this background, it is important to remind ourselves of the implications of GATT and the WTO on the Sugar Protocol. To the extent that the Protocol may be regarded (in WTO terms) as an integral part of the EU 'single regime', and insofar as it ensures maintenance of 'current access' (the Blair House Agreement) in line with the WTO Agreement on Agriculture, then it may be seen to be fully compatible with article XIII of GATT-1994 which ensures 'fair shares' for traditional suppliers. If there are aspects of the Protocol which are not compatible with GATT-1994 and the WTO rules, then the same could also be said of the EU (sugar) single regime as a whole. Moreover, since one of the cardinal principles of the WTO is non-interference in the commercial terms of trade between buyers (in this case, EU sugar buyers) and sellers (ACP sugar sellers), it follows that the WTO should not, nor should it be seen to be, concerned with the guaranteed price of ACP sugar (Julian Price, ED&F Man Sugar Ltd, 9/9/98).

As for world sugar market prices, Hannah argues that the change in the structure of the import market from the late 1980s, when there were reductions in imports by Japan, the United States and the USSR, and the market began to be dominated by developing countries, contributed to stability from 1988 to 1996 (see also International Sugar Journal, 1998, p.162; and Table 5.5). Arguably, this is because LDCs, 'on average, [have] higher price elasticity. Consequently, when prices rose, less was purchased, and vice versa, so that prices became, as we have seen, much more stable; in the average range of 9 to 13 cents/lb' (Hannah, 1998, p. 10; see also FAO, 1986, p. 31 and Figure 5.2). While HFCs have been developed in the USA, it is debatable (at least, in the near future) whether this will have the effect of raising prices, particularly since the EU has instituted regulations on inulin and other competing sweeteners (see Price and Taylor, 1996, p. 66; see also ISO, 1998, pp. 11-13). There are, however, exceptions, such as the drought in Brazil's major centre - south sugar cane region in 2000 which led a recovery of world prices.

Nonetheless, what is clear is that market regulation, in a number of circumstances, has contributed to stabilising prices. For example, in 1995/96, India withheld its massive surplus from the world market, helping to maintain and stabilise world prices - thus acting similarly to previous ISA buffer stock mechanisms. Then again in 1984-87, India had imported 4,165 million tonnes of sugar, helping, not only to absorb massive surpluses and counteracting the impact of the break-up of the Soviet Union, but also maintaining world prices (FAO, 1986, p. 31; Hannah, 1998, p. 16). When there was a decline in cane production in India and Thailand in 1997/98, this was offset by increases in countries such as China and Pakistan. Even when Kenya's 1997/98 production was affected by the El Ninó weather phenomenon, which also saw the damage of sugar crops in Queensland (Australia), the timely joining of Turkey (the fifth largest beet sugar producer in the world) as the 51st member state of the ISO on 21st January 1998 counter-balanced the resulting fall. Admittedly, the drought in Brazil in 2000 did lead to a rise in world prices.

Against this background, how far are Caribbean countries like Barbados, whose quotas were reduced in 1974, and other ACP states exposed to the violent fluctuations in the 'free' market prices, resulting from small changes in quantity free-trade? Fortunately for these countries, the residual 'free' market prices are not representative or meaningful insofar as other Special Arrangements (with generally higher guaranteed prices than free market prices) have tended to counter-balance the effect of the world market to their export earnings. Even during periods of low world prices, as in 1983, sugar generated higher cash returns per hectare than many other crops (Landell Mills Commodities Studies, as cited in Hagelberg, 1987, p. 14). Moreover, as Harris (1986, pp. 3-4) shows, the residual market for disposing 'homeless sugar' had been declining from 1982 (see Table 5.3), albeit disproportionately for different countries, although recent evidence shows that the proportion has risen from 18 per cent in 1990 to 30 per cent of world production in 2000. The 1988-98 period, however, saw relative stability in world prices, itself a result of the complex interplay of institutional, political, social and market conditions (see also Tables 5.4 and 5.5 and Figure 5.3; and personal correspondence with Julian Price, 9/9/98). The extent to which the effects of these factors are being played out in the international scene is beginning to be evident.

Table 5.5 World Production, Consumption and Trade (Millions Tons, Raw Value) 1988-2001

Calendar Year	Production	Consumption	Closing Stocks	Total Trade				World Free Market	
				Exports	Imports	Net Exports	Net Imports	Net Exports	Net Imports
1988	104.6	105.9	44.7	27.4	27.1	23.0	22.7	18.5	18.4
1989	107.2	107.4	44.6	28.0	27.8	22.8	22.6	17.9	17.6
1990	110.7	107.9	47.3	28.5	27.7	24.0	23.2	20.0	19.1
1991	112.3	108.9	52.5	27.3	26.3	22.8	21.8	18.4	17.3
1992	117.3	112.1	56.7	31.8	30.7	25.7	24.6	23.0	22.0
1993	111.4	111.9	52.6	29.3	29.2	24.4	24.3	22.6	22.5
1994	109.6	113.0	49.3	30.1	30.2	24.5	24.5	22.2	22.6
1995	117.5	116.7	48.8	34.7	34.5	28.4	28.1	26.1	25.0
1996	124.2	120.1	52.6	35.4	35.2	29.1	29.0	25.6	26.2
1997	125.1	124.5	53.4	37.0	37.3	30.9	31.2	29.1	29.8
1998	135.0	126.7	-	-	-	-	-	-	-
1999	132.7	129.6	58.3	36.8	36.8	32.3	-	-	-
2000	129.1	132.6	54.8	36.3	36.2	32.7	-	-	-
2001	128.9[1]	131.1[1]	-	-	-	-	-	-	-

Note: [1] = estimates.

Sources: FAO (1997; p. 112); ISO Sugar Yearbook 1996; ISO Yearbook 1998; T. Hannah, Head, Economics and Statistics Division, ISO (correspondence 5.11.98); ISO Quarterly Market Review (June 2001, pp. ii, 8-9, 26-31).

It is interesting to note that sugar, along with bananas and rice, has been excluded from the EBA initiative for which customs duties will be phased out in stages over a three year period between 2006 and 2009 (Europa, 2001). This demonstrates the political significance of sugar within the EU. This also reflects the fact that approximately 250,000 jobs are directly related to sugar in ACPs and the EU port refineries in the UK, France, Portugal and Finland. The nature of the review of the sugar regime, with ACPs constantly appealing to the EU for their views to be considered, also demonstrates the shift of power from the heady days of the negotiations of Lomé I when ACPs often threatened to pull out of the negotiations.

Such a shift in power has also been accompanied by the potential threat of the WTO initiatives to undermine the Sugar Protocol and SPS Agreement. If there is full liberalisation of sugar for LDCs by July 1, 2009, as is proposed, then the main losers are likely to be ACPs such as Mauritius, Fiji, Guyana, Jamaica, Trinidad and Tobago, Belize and Swaziland (see also Table 5.2). Mauritius' immediate position was not helped by severe drought and damage resulting from cyclone Davina in March 1999 (The Sugar Worker, 1999). With a reduction in Mauritius' sugar production in 1999, Guyana was ready to increase its supply to the EU to fill the gap, particularly since it had fortuitously had a record production (in 20 years) in 1999.

Conclusion

The Sugar Protocol is one of many trade agreements which pervade the world economy. While not specifically concerned with stabilising prices, it is part of a regime which aims to guarantee EC farmers an income commensurate with income levels in industry and, consequently, has created within the EC a class of farmers with a high level of political influence on policy formation. Conversely, the ACP are the beneficiaries of an external policy over which they have little control.

Sugar, being a commodity produced by the developed and developing countries, places these countries in direct competition in the world market. The situation of structural surplus which characterises the world market has meant that price levels are generally low, but more importantly, that small producers can have little influence on prices. The EC, on the other hand, as a large world market exporter, has considerable influence on the price level.

As part of the Common organisation of the Market for Sugar in the

EC, the Sugar Protocol extends CAP subsidies to a small number of ACP states. However, while providing higher prices for a select group of developing countries, the operation of the EC sugar regime places ACP producers at a negotiating disadvantage in the determination of the price level and, consequently, the operation of the Protocol.

The economic basis for importing sugar in 1975 was the sugar crisis, and the consequent shortage which left a huge gap in supplies to the UK market. However, ACP sugar is considered an additional supply which exists because of the recognition of the traditional dependency of certain ACP states on sugar exports. Its existence also owes much to an agreement signed at a time when the EC would have been, with the accession of the UK, a deficit producer of sugar. This situation no longer exists and, as a result, the original economic justification for the Protocol is no longer there.

The political basis for the Protocol was the special place of Commonwealth sugar in the British market and in the British government's sugar policy. The CSA was adapted and extended to non Commonwealth developing countries in a special arrangement for ACP sugar in the EC. It proved easier for the EC to have one large multilateral agreement with those developing countries with which it had special concerns, rather than separate bilateral agreements. The EC was thereby pursuing its own development policy and simultaneously facilitating the process of integration with its new members. The Sugar Protocol was thus an unintended outcome of a conflict of interests between ACP cane producers and the CAP, and of a policy crisis within the EC, whereby none of the actors was able to impose its preferred solution (Stevens and Webb, 1983).

In order to maintain the benefits the Sugar Protocol provided in 1975, the ACP have had to defend their position in the EC market in the light of the rapid erosion of preferences arising from policy development in another area. Since 1975 the value of the Protocol to the ACP has been gradually eroded due to increased levels of production in the EC, reduced prices, competition from artificial sweeteners and the decline in the refining capacity of the UK.

The Sugar Protocol continued because the EC sugar regime could adapt to the changes in the international environment, while the economic costs of the Protocol were minimal compared to the alternatives. In other words, the costs of disruption in the EC regime were less than the costs of accommodation and, in the long run, a very small proportion of the benefits of a more co-operative ACP-EC framework.

However, the new Cotonou Agreement, influenced as it is by the need for WTO compatibility, changes the balance of interests so that agreements such as the Sugar Protocol can only continue by virtue of a waiver and face the real threat of being phased out over the next three years.

Notes

1. The formula for indexing movement of costs in the producing countries were meant to ensure that the UK was not underwriting a 'cost-plus' exercise. After 1965, special supplementary payments were brought in to counter Commonwealth countries' dependence on exports of sugar and the depressed world prices which could affect them.

2. The sugar regime, as part of the CAP, takes on board the principles and objectives of the CAP. The CAP binds member governments to act in common over matters of domestic concern, it gives the Commission (especially DG VI, now DG Agriculture) powers of active management not found elsewhere, and it has the most extensive regulatory machinery. However the importance of the CAP politically is disproportionate to the importance of agriculture in the Community. This has a lot to do with the development of extremely effective agricultural producer lobbies who can exert pressure at all levels in the Community machinery (Philip, 1983). Sugar is no exception. Beet producers, and cane refiners, historically exert pressure on sugar policy which other pressure groups lack the force necessary to counter.

3. It is also worth noting that the mechanism of retroactivity seems to have quickly disappeared from the price-fixing method. It was used only twice after the signing of the Lomé Agreement in February 1975; and meant that the price pertaining to the calendar year starting from July could be applied to months before July.

4. The 1934 c.i.f. UK price did fall to £4.17 per long ton which, using the Bank of England index, is equivalent to £75 per metric ton in mid-1985. One word of warning: Bank of England officials regard this price index as a piece of historical research rather than in any way their official view of the effects of inflation. Economists could have long and inconclusive discussions as to whether it is appropriate to use this index in the case of sugar prices. Finally, as it is compiled in terms of sterling, it is doubtful if is appropriate to use it for prices expressed in any other currency e.g. in US dollars (personal correspondence with Colin Campbell, Director of Booker Sugar Limited, 14/6/86).

References

Abbott, G. C. (1989), 'The Commonwealth Sugar Agreement as a model for a New Sugar Protocol', *Development Policy Review*, Vol 7, pp. 343-60.

ACP (1977), Minutes of ACP Ministerial Meeting on Sugar, Barbados.

ACP (1977), Minutes of the negotiations concerning the guaranteed prices applicable in 1977/8, Brussels 9/6/77.

ACP (1985), 'The Sugar Protocol in ACP-EEC Relations: the case for a reaffirmation of commitment', ACP/63/079/85 Brussels.

ACP London Sugar Group (1996), Aide Memoire on ACP Sugar, April.

ACP London Sugar Group (1998), Aide Memoire on ACP Sugar, January.

Agra Europe's CAP Monitor (1989), 'Preferential sugar import quotas', Appendix 7, January 11.

Albert, B. (1976), *An essay on the Peruvian sugar industry 1880-1920, and the Letters of Ronald Gordon, Administrator of the British Sugar Company in Canete, 1914-1920*, The School of Social Studies, University of East Anglia, Norwich, UK.

Albert, B. (1984), 'The labour force on Peru's sugar plantations 1820-1930: A Survey', in *Crisis and change in the international sugar economy 1886-1914*, Bill Albert and Adrian Graves (eds.), ISC Press, Norwich and Edinburgh.

Albert, B. (1988), 'The Peruvian sugar industry 1918-1939: Response to the world crisis', in *The world sugar economy in war and depression, 1914-40*, Bill Albert and Adrian Graves (eds.), Routledge, London.

Albert, B., and Graves, A. (1984), 'Introduction', in *Crisis and change in the international sugar economy 1860-1914*, ISC Press, Norwich and Edinburgh.

Albert, B., and Graves, A. (1988), 'Introduction' in *The world sugar economy in war and depression, 1914-40*, Bill Albert and Adrian Graves (eds.), Routledge, London.

Barclays Review (1984), Food Commodity Prices (November).

Beechert, E. D. (1988), 'Technology and the plantation labour supply: The case of Queensland, Hawaii, Louisiana and Cuba', in *The world sugar economy in war and depression, 1914-40*, Bill Albert and Adrian Graves (eds.), Routledge: London.

Boomgaard, P. (1988), 'Treacherous cane: The Java sugar industry between 1914 and 1940', in *The World Sugar Economy in War and Depression, 1914-40*, Bill Albert and Adrian Graves (eds.), Routledge, London.

Brown, M. B. (1972), *Essays on imperialism*, Spokesman Books, Nottingham.

Castle, B. (1975), 'Sugar saga - sweet nothing from Europe', *The Guardian* (June 3).

CEC (1994), 'Integration of Developing countries into the International Trading System: Role of GSP, 1995-2000', COM (94) 212 final. Brussels.

CEC (1999), 'Consequences for ACP countries of applying to the GSP', Joint analysis by EC and ACP experts. CE/TFN/GCE3/29-EU. Brussels.

Chalmin, Ph. G. (1984), 'The important trends in sugar diplomacy before 1914', in *Crisis and change in the international sugar economy 1860-1914*, Bill Albert and Adrian Graves (eds.), ISA Press: Norwich and Edinburgh.

Commonwealth Secretariat (1983), 'The Challenge to Cane Sugar in the 1980s', *Report of a seminar held at the Commonwealth Institute*, London.

Courier, The (1975), Lomé Dossier, EEC/ACP No. 31 - Special (March).

Courier, The (1979), Lomé II Dossier, ACP/EEC, Special Issue No.58 (November).

Courier, The (1982), 'Sugar', Dossier, *The Courier*, No.75 (September-October).

Courier, The (1984), ACP-EEC, 'Consultative Assembly: Last Chance to Influence Negotiations', *The Courier*, No. 88 (November -December).

Courier, The (1985), Third ACP-EEC Convention (Signed at Lomé on 8 December 1984), No. 89 - Special Issue (January-February).

Courier, The (1986), 'ACP-EEC trade', *The Courier*, No. 98 (July-August).

Courier, The (1989), 'Lomé IV - The ACP negotiating position', *The Courier*, No. 113 (January-February).

Courier, The (2000), Special Issue, ACP-EU Partnership Agreement signed in Cotonou on 23 June, Brussels.

Cutajar, M. Z., and Franks, A. (1967), *The less Developed Countries in World Trade: A reference handbook*, The Overseas Development Institute Ltd, London.

Czarnikow, C. (1986), Annual Review, C. Czarnikow Ltd, London.

Delson, R. M. (1984), 'Sugar production for the nineteenth century British market:

Rethinking the roles of Brazil and the British West Indies', in *Crisis and change in the international sugar economy 1860-1914*, Bill Albert and Adrian Graves (eds.), ISC Press, Norwich and Edinburgh.

Dodoo, C., and Kuster, R. (1977), 'The Road to Lomé', in *The Lomé Convention and a New International Economic Order*, F. A. M. Altingvon Gesaud (ed.) Leyden, A.W. Sijthoff.

Edwards, J. (1983), 'World Sugar Market: Why Europe's Rivals are Sour', *Financial Times* (August 17).

EEC (1974), 'The Common Organisation of the Sugar Market', EEC Council Regulation 3330/74, OJ 17.

Erlichman, J. (1983), 'Bitter News for World's Sugar Producers: Coca Cola has switched to a new kind of sweetener', *The Guardian*, (April 27).

Europa (2001), Europa.eu.int/comm/trade/miti/devel/index_en.htm, 13/02/01.

European Parliament (EP) (1974), 'On the future Sugar Protocol of the Commonwealth with particular reference to imports of sugar from the Developing Countires and in the light of the Commission memorandum of 12 July 1973', *Working Document* 32/74.

FAO (1978), *Commodity Review and Outlook 1977-79*, FAO, UN.

FAO (1979), *Commodity Review and Outlook 1979-80*, FAO, UN.

FAO (1985), 'Sugar: major trade and stabilization issues in the eighties', *FAO Economic and Social Development Paper*, Part No. 50.

FAO (1986), *Commodity Review and Outlook 1985-86*, FAO, UN.

FAO (1997), *FAO Quarterly Bulletin of Statistics*, Vol. 10, Nos 3/4.

Gonzales, M. J. (1984), 'Economic Crisis, Chinese workers and the Peruvian sugar planters 1875-1900: A case of labour and the national elite', in *Crisis and Change in the International Sugar Economy, 1860-1914*, Bill Albert and Adrian Graves (eds.), ISC Press, Norwich and Edinburgh.

Gruhn, I. V. (1976), 'The Lomé Convention: Inching Towards Interdependence', *International Organisation*, Vol. 30, No. 2 (Spring).

Guy, D. J. (1984), 'Sugar industries at the periphery of the world market: Argentina, 1860-1914', in *Crisis and change in the international sugar economy 1860-1914*, Bill Albert and Adrian Graves (eds.), ISC Press, Norwich and Edinburgh.

Hagelberg, G. B. (1974), 'The Caribbean Sugar Industries: Constraints and Opportunities', *Occasional Paper No. 3*, Antilles Research Program, Yale University.

Hagelberg, G. B. (1975), 'Sugar', in *Commodity Trade of the Third World*, Cheryl Payer (ed.), Macmillan, London.

Hagelberg, G. B. (1987), 'The free world sugar market and the EEC sugar regime', Paper presented to the *Regional Seminar on sugar workers*, University of Mauritius (9-13 February), Sugar World, ICCSASW, Toronto, Canada.

Hannah, A .C. (1982), 'Imbalance in the World Sugar Economy: Some ideas about causes and remedies in the context of a New International Sugar Agreement', *F.O. Licht's International Sugar Report*, 114:581-89.

Hannah, A. C. (1998), 'The World Sugar Market and Reform', *PROSI Magazine (International Relations)*, No. 348 (January). http://prosi.intnet.mu/348jan/hann348.htm (first published in F.O. Licht's Sugar Newsletter, Vol. 129, No. 31, October 17, 1997).

Hardy, T. (1987), 'Report from the United Kingdom', Paper presented to the *Regional Seminar on Sugar workers*, University of Mauritius (9-13 February), Sugar World, ICCSASW, Toronto, Canada.

Harris, S. (1973), 'British sugar market in an international context', in *World sugar markets in a state of flux*, Agricultural Trade Paper No. 4, Simon Harris and Ian Smith (eds.), Trade Policy Research Centre: London.

Harris, S. (1981), 'Recent trends in protectionism in the world sugar market', *Secretariat*

Market Report No. 94, Group of Latin American and Caribbean Sugar Exporting Countries (GEP LACEA).

Harris, S. (1985), 'Review of the EC sugar market', *Report to the World Bank.*

Harris, S. (1986), 'Some current issues in the world sugar economy', Address to a Conference on Crisis and change in the international sugar economy, University of East Anglia, Norwich, UK (September 1).

Harris, S. (1987), 'Current Issues in the World Sugar Economy', *Food Policy* Vol. 12, No. 2, May.

Harris, S., and Hagelberg, G. B. (1975), 'Effects of the Lomé Convention on the World's Cane-Sugar Producers', *ODI Review*, No. 2.

Harris, S. and Josling, T. (1975), 'Can world commodity prices be explained?', *National Westminster Bank Review* (August).

Harris, S., and Smith, I. (1973), *World sugar markets in a state of flux*, Agricultural Trade Paper No. 4, Trade Policy Research Centre, London.

Harris, S., Swinbank, A., and Wilkinson, G. (1983), *The Food and Farm Policies of the European Union*, John Wiley, Chichester.

Harris, S., and Tangermann, S. (1993), 'A Review of the EC Sugar Market', in *The Economics and Politics of World Sugar Policies*, S. V. Marks and K. E. Maskus (eds.) University of Michigan Press, Ann Arbor, Michigan.

Hoffmeyer, B. (1981), 'Trends in EEC Agricultural Policy: Possible Consequences for the Developing Countries', *CDR Research Paper A.81.5*, Copenhagen.

Hoffmeyer, B. (1982), 'The EEC's Common Agricultural Policy and the ACP', *CRD Research Paper No. 2*, Copenhagen.

House of Lords (1980), 'EEC Sugar Policy', 44th Report of the Select Committee of the EC Session 79/80.

Huberman, L., and Sweezy, P. M. (1983), *Cuba: Anatomy of a Revolution*, Monthly Review Press, New York.

IDS (1998), 'CAP Reforms: Will Developing Countries Benefit?' *IDS Policy Briefing*, Issue II (February).

International Sugar Journal (1998), Vol. C, Issue No.1992, April.

ISO (1996), *Sugar Year Book*, International Sugar Organisation, London.

ISO (1998), *Quarterly Market Review*, March.

ISO (various years), *Sugar Year Book*, International Sugar Organisation, London.

Josling, T. (1979), 'The European Community Agricultural Policies and the Interest of Developing Countries', *ODI Review*, No. 1.

Koch, T. (1989), 'The Sugar Protocol: An Appraisal', *Intereconomics* 24, pp. 293-7.

Koester, U., and Schmitz, P. M. (1982), 'The EC sugar market policy and developing countries', *European Review of Agricultural Economics* 9 (pp. 183-204).

Laidlaw, K. (1983), 'The Sugar Protocol: Room for Improvement', *Lomé Briefing No. 12.*

Landell Mills Commodity Studies (1984), *Sugar Quarterly*, November.

Leroy, O. (1980), 'The question of commodities in the North-South dialogue', *Europe Information Development*, No. X/294/80 EN, Commission of the European Communities.

Liaison News (2000), No 10, CLONG, Brussels.

Licht, F. O. (1983b), 'World Sugar Balances', *F.O. Licht's International SugarReport.*

Lister, M. (1988), *The European Community and the Developing World*, Gower, Aldershot.

MAFF (1988), *The EEC Sugar Regime.* HMSO, London.

MAFF (1989), Speech to ACP Sugar Conferences, Brussels 16/9/89.

McDonald, S. (1996), 'Reform of the EU's Sugar Policies and the ACP Countries', *Development Policy Review*, Vol. 14, No. 2 (June).

McGregor, A. M. (1978), 'The Lomé Convention and the ACP sugar exporters: The political economy of conflicting policies', *Ph.D Thesis*, Cornell University (May).

Mahler, V. A. (1981), 'Britain, the European Community and the Developing Commonwealth: Dependence, Interdependence, and the Political Economy of Sugar', *International Organisation*, Vol. 35, No. 3 (Summer).

Mahler, V. A. (1984), 'The political economy of North-South commodity bargaining: the case of the International Sugar Agreement', *International Organisation*, Vol. 38, No. 4 (Autumn).

Moyes, A. (1987), Common ground: How changes in the Common Agricultural Policy affect the Third World Poor, Oxfam, Oxford.

Moynagh, M. (1977), 'The Negotiation of the Commonwealth Sugar Agreement, 1949-1951', Journal of Commonwealth and Comparative Political Studies 15 (July).

Nagano, Y. (1988), 'The oligopolistic structure of the Philippine sugar industry during the Great Depression', in *The world sugar economy in war and depression, 1914-40*, Bill Albert and Adrian Graves (eds.), Routledge, London.

Ndhlovu, T. P. (1990), 'How can the movements of sugar cane cutters' wage rates be explained? A comparative study drawing on the experiences of Barbados, Fiji and Mauritius', *Ph.D Thesis*, University of East Anglia (February).

Ndhlovu, T.P. (1999), 'The determination of sugar export prices: Post war experiences, with reference to the EU/ACP Sugar Protocol', *MMU Discussion Paper*, No. 9907 (July).

North-Coombes, M. D. (1988), 'Struggles in the cane fields: Small cane growers in Mauritius, 1921-1937', in *The world sugar economy in war and depression, 1914-1940*, Bill Albert and Adrian Graves (eds.), Routledge, London.

The North London Haslemere Group (1973), *Sugar today, Jam tomorrow?* Haselmere Declaration Group and Third World First, London and Oxon.

O'Connor, J. (1973), *The Fiscal Crisis of the State*, St. Martin's Press, New York.

Official Journal of the European Communities (1987), Statement by the Commission concerning Article 7 (4) of Protocol 7 on ACP sugar annexed to the Third ACP-EEC Lomé Convention, No. C278/2, October 16.

Perkins, J. (1988), 'The German beet-sugar industry and the Nazi Machtergreifung of 1933', in *The World sugar economy in war and depression 1914-40*, Bill Albert and Adrian Graves (eds.), Routledge, London.

Persaud, B. (1973), 'An economic study of the Barbados sugar industry', *Ph.D. Thesis*, University of Reading, Department of Agricultural Economics and Management (August 31).

Philip, A. B. (ed.) (1983), *Institutions and the Politics of the European Community*, Frances Pinter, London.

Pigman, G. A. (1997), 'Hegemony and trade liberalisation policy: Britain and the Brussels Sugar Convention of 1902', *Review of International Studies*, Vol. 23, No. 2 (April).

Pollitt, B. (1988), 'The Cuban sugar economy in the 1930s', in *The world sugar economy in war and depression, 1914-40*, Bill Albert and Adrian Graves (eds.), Routledge, London.

Poole, J., Eglin, R., and Ritchie, B. (1974), 'The sugar shambles and who shambled it', *The Sunday Times* (November 10).

Post, K. (1978), *Arise Ye Starvelings: The Jamaican Labour Rebellion of 1938 and its Aftermath*, Martinus Nijhoff, The Hague/Boston/London.

Prasad, S. and Akram-Lodhi, A. H. (1998), 'Fiji and the Sugar Protocol: A case for trade-based development co-operation', *Development Policy Review*, Vol. 16, No. 1 (March).

Price, J., and Taylor, R. (1996), *European Union Sugar: The EU sugar policy, the agrimonetary system, GATT and the WTO*, ED & F Man Sugar Ltd, London.

Public Records Office (PRO) (1959), Memo by the Chancellor of the Exchequer, Cab (59)

27. 20 February.

Ramphal, S. S. (1983), Rekindling 'The Spirit of Lomé', *Lomé Briefing No.1.*

Ravenhill, J. (1985), *Collective Clientelism: The Lomé Conventions and North-South Relations*, Columbia University Press: New York.

Richardson, D. (1986), 'The policy Europe should pursue is to control production so as to avoid having to dump surpluses on to world markets', *Big Farm Weekly* (June 19).

Richardson, P. (1984), 'The Natal sugar industry in the nineteenth century', in *Crisis and change in the international sugar economy 1860-1914*, Bill Albert and Adrian Graves (eds.), ISC Press, Norwich and Edinburgh.

Roca, S. (1976), *Cuban Economic Policy and Ideology: The Ten Million Ton Sugar Harvest*, Professional Papers in International Studies, 02-44, Sage: Beverly Hills.

Routh, G. (ed) (1988), *Mauritius Sugar Authority: Sugar Industry Efficiency Study 1988 - Component 5, Manpower and Labour Productivity*, Food Studies Group, Oxford, UK (March).

Schiffman, C. (1975), 'A Negotiation and a Convention', *The Courier No.31 - Special Issue* (March).

Schnakenbourg, C. (1984), 'From the sugar estate to central factory: The industrial revolution in the Caribbean (1840-1905)', in *Crisis and change in the international sugar economy 1860-1914*, Bill Albert and Adrian Graves (eds.) ISC Press, Norwich and Edinburgh.

Smith, I. (1973), 'Commonwealth sugar exports and the European Community', in *World sugar markets in a state of flux*, Agricultural Trade Paper No. 4, Simon Harris and Ian Smith (eds.), Trade Policy Research Centre, London.

Southgate, J. (1984), *The Commonwealth Sugar Agreement 1951-74*, C. Czarnikov Ltd, London.

Stevens, C. and Webb (1983), *The Political Economy of Sugar: A window on the CAP, Policy Making in the EC*, John Wiley & Sons, Sussex.

The Sugar Worker (1999), Vol. 1, No. 3 (September).

Symrecsanyi, T. (1988), 'Growth and crisis of the Brazilian sugar industry, 1914-1939', in *The world sugar economy in war and depression, 1914-40*, Bill Albert and Adrian Graves (eds.) Routledge, London.

Thomas, H. (1971), *Cuba or The Pursuit of Freedom*, Harper & Row, New York.

UNCTAD (1987), ISA, 1987, UN Sugar Conference, 1987.

UNCTAD (1992), ISA, 1992, UN Sugar Conference, 1992.

Whiteman, K. (1998), 'Africa, the ACP and the Europe: The lessons of 25 years', *Development Policy Review*, Vol. 16, No. 1 (March).

6 The Rum Protocol

STEPHEN DEARDEN

The Rum Protocol was distinct from the other Protocols in that there is no list of specific ACP signatories, instead it was open to all ACP states, it has also been the first to be abandoned.

The Rum Protocol of the Lomé Conventions (Protocol 6) has been of particular importance for the Caribbean ACP States. ACP rum exports to the EU have risen significantly since Lomé I, from €21.6m in 1976 to €251.8 m. in 1998 (Commodity Code 2208), supplying 68 per cent of all EU rum imports. Although Fiji, Madagascar, Mozambique and Mauritius are all rum producers they do not export to the EU. Instead the EU's imports are provided by the Commonwealth Caribbean (Table 6.1). Most of these imports originate in Trinidad and Tobago, the Bahamas, Guyana, Jamaica and Barbados. For the Bahamas and Trinidad and Tobago rum exports make a significant contribution to their export earnings - 37 per cent and 30 per cent respectively in 1998. CARICOM as a whole exported rum to a value of €248.9 m. (13 per cent of total EU exports) in 1998. It is estimated that the industry employees 10,000 people in the region.

Although an internationally competitive industry, the relatively small size of the domestic market means that access to the EU is essential if it is to fully exploit economies of scale and reduce unit costs to an acceptable level.

While there are no producers of rum within the mainland EU, Guadeloupe and Martinique in the Caribbean, and the Indian Ocean territory of Reunion (Overseas Departments of France (DOMs)), are competitors. The definition of rum as an agricultural product and the protectionism of the Rum Protocol has been driven by the desire of the French government to protect its DOM producers from foreign competition. Rum represented 9 per cent of Martinique's exports in the 1990s and the distillation and bottling of rum accounts for a major part of industrial employment in the island. The EU supports their production of rum through exemptions from Community excise duties and through

Table 6.1 Rum Exports to the EU

	1992 € Million	1992 % Export Earnings	1998 € Million	1998 % Export Earnings
Bahamas	30.3	13.5	118.8	37
Barbados	1.5	3.9	3.8	7
Guyana	7.8	5.3	5.1	3
Jamaica	7.2	2.6	9.5	2
Trinidad & Tobago	73.6	42	113.9	30

Source: Eurostat.

subsidies. There are two measures supporting the sugar cane and rum sectors, flat-rate aid per hectare for cane growers and aid for processing sugar cane into agricultural rum (COM(2000)147). The flat rate aid was intended to improve planting - with the introduction of new varieties - bring down the average age of the crop and improve yields. 54,538 hectares (ha.) were eligible for assistance with new planting (1992-98), with 13,383 ha. in Guadeloupe and 2,853 in Martinique qualifying. Land improvement was also funded, the removal of stones allowing mechanised cutting. 1,666 ha. in Guadeloupe received assistance and 342 ha. in Martinique. The EC funded 60 per cent of the cost of the scheme (EEC 1487/92) which began in 1992 and was intended to run for seven years. However the scheme took longer to implement than expected and France sought an extension until the end of 1999. At the end of scheme almost 80 per cent of the area of sugar cultivation in Guadeloupe had been replanted and 70 per cent in Martinique, raising yields by 8 per cent and 20 per cent respectively.

Of more significance has been the subsidy to rum distillers. Under Regulation EEC 3763/91 distillers who paid a defined minimum price to sugar cane producers received a subsidy that, by 1997, was set at €64.22 per hectolitre of pure alcohol (EC 2598/95). The overall subsidy was limited to 75,600 hectolitres (hl.), the average quantity produced between 1987 and 1990, and allocated between France's four DOMs. Martinique was allocated a quota of 60,230 hl. (1992-98), Guadeloupe 14,200 hl. and French Guiana 778 hl. Martinique only claimed subsidies for 56,461 hl., but both French Guiana (Guyane) and Guadeloupe exhausted the sums available. This aid to the DOM's rum industry has been seen as essential to sustain it in the face of competition from the ACP rum producers of the

Caribbean whose sugar cane costs are lower. The distillery closures that had preceded its introduction in 1992 have now ceased.

For the ACP producers the Rum Protocol allowed duty-free access to the EU market for all ACPs up to a tariff quota expressed in terms of hectolitres (hl.) of pure alcohol. From the commencement of Lomé I until the establishment of the single European market in 1993, this overall quota was allocated between the Member States of the Community. This was calculated on the basis of the largest annual quantities imported into a country in the last three years, with an additional increase of 40 per cent for the UK and 13 per cent for other markets (Table 6.2). By far the largest market for rum imports was the United Kingdom, supplied predominantly by the Commonwealth Caribbean producers, and this was reflected in the relative size of the quotas. However to protect the French DOM suppliers re-export between the UK and the rest of the Community was prevented by Regulation 1464/76.

Table 6.2 Rum Quotas

	1975/76		**1976/77**		**1977/78**		**1978/79**	
	Quota hl. ('000)	**Take-up %**	**Quota hl. ('000)**	**Take-up %**	**Quota hl. ('000)**	**Take-up %**	**Quota hl. ('000)**	**Take-up %**
Benelux	3.5	100	4.8	100	5.9	87	6.0	97
Denmark	2.9	67	2.7	78	4.0	39	3.7	39
Germany	26.0	81	24.6	94	24.0	87	24.7	100
France	6.0	100	12.0	41	11.4	48	9.0	39
Ireland	1.0	84	1.0	89	1.0	68	1.0	49
Italy	0.6	35	0.5	39	0.6	45	0.4	100
UK	128.0	49	125.4	63	126.0	66	116.9	89

Source: Report of the ACP-EEC Council of Ministers (April 1976-Feb 1980).

Given the competitive advantages of the Commonwealth Caribbean suppliers the size of the quotas was a continuing cause of friction as, more importantly, was the prevention of re-export within the Community. Attempts to challenge the legality of this restriction under the Treaty of Rome proved futile, while the accuracy of the statistics which formed the basis for the rolling quota calculations remained a subject of dispute. The ACP producers also challenged the small size of the quotas for their non-traditional markets, which made it impossible to justify a significant export drive in these under-developed areas. The ACPs also alleged non-tariff barriers were operating in some markets, especially Germany, where obstacles to the issuing of import licenses appeared to be being employed to favour Brazilian suppliers. As a result of these difficulties the initial take-up of quotas was often limited. Thus although the Rum Protocol preserved the major United Kingdom market for the ACP suppliers it also inhibited their expansion into other new and expanding markets in the Community.

In response to these criticisms the Commission proposed the ending of the controls upon resale in the Community as part of the revisions leading to Lomé II. An overall ceiling would be introduced based upon imports in 1978 and increased by a fixed quantity each year thereafter (equal to 5 per cent in the first year). For the UK government these proposals were unacceptable since they represented a significant reduction in the rate of growth in the quotas which had occurred under Lomé I and they were rejected by the French as a threat to their DOM producers. As a result the outcome was a continuation of the existing national quota allocation system but with an increase of 18 per cent per annum for the ACPs non-traditional markets. It was to be the advent of the single European market that was to herald the end of the compartmentalisation of the EU rum market.

By 1993 the total quota for the EU was set at 224,000 hectolitres (hl.) and it was increased by 20,000 hl. for 1994 and 1995. However a new regime was introduced in 1996 after the mid-term review of Lomé IV and sustained lobbying by the Caribbean producers. Quotas on light rum from ACP suppliers were abolished, but retained for dark rum (defined as rum with a content of volatile substances other than ethyl and methyl alcohol equal to or exceeding 225 grams per hectolitre of pure alcohol). Therefore protectionism was to continue on dark rum until 2000, after which this quota was also to be abolished. As part of the settlement of these negotiations the ACP States withdrew their objections to the extension of EU assistance to the French DOM producers, recognising that most of their exports were only supplying the French market. The quotas were set at 58,000 hl. for 1996, 61,000 hl. for 1997, 64,000 hl. for 1998 and 67,000 hl. for 1999 (Regulation 2599/95). The removal of tariffs on light rum particularly benefited Trinidad and Tobago which had a strong position in the light rum market (Bacardi). The whole industry, in anticipation of the removal of quotas and the general opening up of the European market, began to expand its sales of both bulk and branded products in non-traditional EU markets, such as Germany and the Netherlands.

Before the negotiations to determine the successor agreement to Lomé IV could come to fruition the EU had already signed the death warrant of the Rum Protocol. Despite the commitment to consultation with the ACP States under the existing Convention, the EU unilaterally agreed to open up its market for spirits. For in 1997, at the Singapore WTO Ministerial Meeting of the Uruguay Round, as a 'sweetener' in the negotiations related to information technology, a 'zero-for-zero' tariff agreement was reached between the EU and the USA covering distilled spirits. This committed the two parties to the gradual abolition of all tariffs and quotas on distilled spirits by 2003, but included a special annex covering rum in the form of a 'Memorandum of Understanding'. As well as some transitional protection for ACP imports, this provided for a residual duty of €0.6 per cent volume per hl. on bulk shipments (in containers greater than 2 litres), with an additional duty of €3.2 per cent volume per hl. on branded and bottled products. However without an extension of the Lomé concessions ACP exporters would also have faced this duty from 2000.

For the ACPs this agreement was a major threat to their industry. In response, in March 1997, the ACP rum producers sought the support of the ACP/EU Joint Assembly, which called upon the Community to honour the commitments given under IV, to grant a ten year transition period and to ensure that the ACP producers interests were not adversely affected by any agreement with third countries. However the EU made it clear that it was not prepared to consider special arrangements for a single commodity outside of the general provisions for a successor to Lomé IV. Subsequently the EU's General Affairs Council confirmed the 'zero-for-zero' tariff agreement with the US (97/360/EC), but reiterated that it 'will not change in any way the terms of access enjoyed by the ACP rum exporters to the Community market, in the framework of the Lomé Convention... and do not prejudge the future of this regime after the said Convention's expiry in the year 2000'. They recognised 'the likely impact of the EU-US agreement on the ACP exports of rum to the EU market and confirm that this will be taken fully into account in any future negotiations and arrangements relating to the rum sector' (24th May 1997, Declaration on Rum). They also recall the provisions of Annex XXIX of the Convention which notes that the 'Community is conscious of the need to ensure…the maintenance of the competitive position of the ACP States where their advantages on the Community market are affected by measures relating to general trade liberalisation. The Community declares its willingness, whenever ACP States bring to its attention any specific case, jointly to study specific appropriate action with a view to safeguarding the ACP's interests'. In practice it marked the end of the Rum Protocol.

However its termination may not necessarily be against the interests of the ACP rum producers. Since the first Lomé Convention the benefits have been questioned. The Caribbean producers have always been viewed as highly competitive suppliers to the EU market, with the quota limit regarded as protection for the French DOMs or third party suppliers. The major objection to the ending of the preferential access arrangements for the EU market has centred upon the issue of the fairness of the competition from other subsidised international suppliers, such as the US Virgin Islands, the Philippines and Brazil. It has been estimated by Berg (1998) that 87 per cent of global alcohol production is subsidised.

Thus the West Indies Rum and Spirits Producers Association (WIRSPA) - representing the rum distillers and suppliers from Guyana, the Bahamas, Jamaica, Barbados, Trinidad and Tobago, St. Lucia, Antigua and the Dominican Republic - continued to lobby the EU to honour its commitments, given at the time of the mid-term review of Lomé IV, to abolish all quotas and tariffs on traditional ACP rum exports by 2000, and to guarantee that it would not extend duty-free access beyond the concessions given under the EU/US 'Memorandum of Understanding' to any additional third countries. There was concern that any extensions of the General System of Preferences, offered by the EU to non-ACP developing countries, would further enhance competition, in particular that South Africa or Cuba might be offered favourable access, or that the Millenium Round of the WTO would result in further reductions in the residual tariff. The threat of imports of 'verschnitt' type rum from Central and Eastern Europe, especially from possible new members of the Community, was also recognised. To address these problems WIRSPA also sought an increase in the residual transitional duties on competing rum imports, at least equal to the rate of inflation between 1997 and 2003 and, most importantly, the provision of additional technical and financial assistance to their rum producers to prepare for the free market.

As distilleries in the Caribbean have only small local markets they are dependent upon a significant export trade to achieve sufficient economies of scale to remain competitive. But they have also concentrated, historically, upon the bulk rum market, which is particularly price sensitive. Thus any erosion of their EU market share in the face of increased subsidised international competition could be disastrous for the future of the industry. The solution that WIRSPA has identified is a strategy for the development of a portfolio of local brands, marketed within a legally defined generic 'Caribbean Rum' title, to exclude products supplied from other parts of the world including Central and Eastern Europe. To assist they also sought the support of the Community by restricting the term rum, both light and traditional, to those spirits which conform to EEC Regulation 1576/89. This change from a commodity based industry to higher-margin brand-based production will take some time and hence WIRSPA proposed a transitional period of 15 years. During this period they sought €5 million of EU funds to assist in the modernisation of production plant - including addressing the problem of effluent treatment - the development of the generic 'Caribbean Rum' brand, undertaking market studies, training staff and building WIRSPA as an institution. But almost uniquely amongst ACP industries faced with demands for trade liberalisation, the EU has declined to provide any additional earmarked assistance, instead arguing that the funds should be allocated from existing National or Regional Indicative Programmes. Such an allocation has been a possibility under Lomé since its inception but the Caribbean producers have always found it difficult to access these funds in the past.

The threat of US competition has finally brought the ACP and DOM producers together to defend their interests. At a meeting in Barbados in July 1997 WIRSPA and CIRT-DOM reach an accord endorsing WIRSPA's objectives and offering WIRSPA's support for a continuation of the level of subsidies and preferences offered to the DOM industry. The maintenance of a privileged French market for DOM produced rum was seen as a compromise worth accepting for WIRSPA, given the broader challenges they were all now facing.

'If the EU does not continue to offer special arrangements for ACP rum after 2000' argued WIRSPA (1997), 'then the likelihood is that the ACP market share will rapidly attenuate as non-traditional producers enter the market, free of restriction. If this happens the EU will have halted conclusively the ability of one of the few agro-based industries in the Caribbean to improve its market share in Europe. In doing so it will have also undercut the viability of one of the few indigenous industries able to produce increasing flows of foreign currency into the Caribbean and expand job creation in the region and will have used the Lomé Convention for a purpose opposite to that intended'.

Although this concerted lobbying was unsuccessful in preventing the ratification of the EU/US Memorandum, it did succeed in extracting from the EU the undertakings that WIRSPA had been seeking to improve the transitional arrangements. Most importantly it resulted in a Joint Declaration on Rum (Declaration XXV) in the Cotonou Agreement. This recognised the importance of the industry to employment, export earnings and government revenues for some ACP States and its international competitive potential. It acknowledged the general commitment given by the General Affairs Council in 1997 to fully take into account in future negotiations the impact of the EU/US deal and the need to encourage the diversification of exports away from low value-added bulk sales. To this end the EU committed itself to the removal of all tariffs and quota restrictions on rum imports from ACP States. In regard to third country imports it undertook to ensure fair competition, guaranteed that ACP rum will not be disadvantaged or discriminated against in the EU market and to consult on any derogations from the product requirements/definition embodied in Regulation 1576/1989. Although not committing itself to indexation of the remaining duties on non-ACP rum under the Memorandum of Understanding, as requested by WIRSPA, the issue was to be examined. In terms of financial assistance the EU undertook to prepare an integrated sector-specific programme, which would focus upon enhancing the competitiveness of existing exporters and assist in the diversification out of bulk sales through the development of regional or country brands and appropriate marketing. Funding would also assist producers to meet the new environmental standards for effluent treatment. The finance would be provided both on a regional and national basis and, initially, from unallocated EDF resources. A joint working party was also established to monitor progress on these issues and to provide a forum for consultations on any bilateral or multilateral decisions affecting the rum industry. Most significantly it will be able to address any proposal for further extensions of tariff reductions under the WTO, GSP or arising from the accession of new members to the Community.

The future for the ACP rum sector ultimately depends upon the dynamism of the individual companies themselves. Whatever arrangements are made between governments the future of the industry depends upon the performance of individual firms and the industry's own success in restructuring and marketing. The EU's sectoral funding should be crucial in this process, but the substantial Investment Facility, also created under the Cotonou Agreement and designed specifically to foster the development of the private sector, may also make a significant contribution. The EU's role in assisting rum companies remains central, as other international donors are reluctant to fund restructuring in an industry that appears relatively successful and they often have a preference for government-to-government arrangements. The rum industry of the Caribbean may thus become a case study in the ability of the private sector in developing countries to attract investment.

Although the institutional framework for the Caribbean producers to lobby in defence of their interests has been established, the future outcome of such negotiations remains as uncertain as ever. It is unlikely that the ACP producers will be caught as unaware as they were with the EU/US Memorandum of Understanding, but consultation is not power. In the context of broader international negotiations, such as the forthcoming Millennium Round of the WTO or the negotiations for accession to the EU of States in Central and Eastern Europe, it is unlikely that the interests of Caribbean rum producers will be high up on the agenda or allowed to obstruct complex final settlements. The opening up of the Community market has begun and the ACP producers have accepted this reality. They have sensibly focused upon the transitional arrangements and the development of an industry strategy that will allow them to meet international competition. They have one great advantage over the other commodity producers that have been considered in this book, on a proverbial international 'level playing field' they have the potential to be winners.

References

Berg, C. (1998), *Towards a World Ethanol Market*? F. O. Licht Commodity Analysis.

Davenport, M., Hewitt A., & Koning A. (1995) *Europe's Preferred Partners? The Lomé Countries in World Trade*, Overseas Development Institute, London.

Dunlop, A. (1999), What Future for Lomé's Commodity Protocols? ECDPM Discussion Paper 5, Maastricht.

ECDPM (1999), The Future of Lomé's Commodity Protocols : Fiddling While Rum Burns?, Lomé Negotiating Brief 6.

McQueen et al. (1998), ACP-EU Trade and Aid Co-operation Post Lomé IV, EAD Economic Paper, London.

Ravenhill, J. (1985), *Collective Clientelism: The Lomé Conventions and North-South Relations*, Colombia University Press, New York.

West Indies Rum and Spirit Producers Association (1997), Submission to the House of Commons, International Development Committee.

7 Conclusion

STEPHEN DEARDEN

The common themes running throughout this analysis of the Commodity Protocols of the EU are their particular economic importance to some of the countries of the Commonwealth Caribbean and their demise in the face of the challenge by the United States, under the auspices of the WTO. The historic political and economic post-colonial Commonwealth links of the United Kingdom have rapidly weakened, firstly as the country was integrated more fully into the European Community, and then as the EU itself deepened its economic relations; especially with the creation of the single market, which significantly enhanced the role of the Commission in international trade negotiations. The context of these international negotiations has also changed with the replacement of the GATT by the WTO, which has strengthened the latters role in the regulation of international trade, exposed weaknesses in the ability of smaller states to defend their interests in its deliberations and hastened the movement towards free trade and globalisation.

For the European Community as a whole, the last few decades has seen a comparable weakening in the priority accorded to the interests of the African Caribbean and Pacific group of developing countries. A product of colonial relations, principally of France and the United Kingdom, the Lomé Conventions sustained a special relationship. However the shifting political priorities of the EU has seen increasing proportions of its aid funding directed to the countries of Central and Eastern Europe, while the entry of Spain and Portugal into the Community has also focused the EU much more strongly upon South America. This has been reflected in the increasing proportion of EU aid which is dispensed through the general budget rather than the European Development Funds associated with the ACP Conventions.

The development policy of the EU, as for many Western governments, has been freed from the global political imperatives of 'cold war' rivalries, allowing a fundamental reconsideration of its aims and objectives. A 'poverty focus' has finally emerged as one of the principal criteria for evaluating the effectiveness of EU policy and yet the ACP group, with its historical antecedents, excludes many of the world's least developed countries. Even within the Commonwealth the countries of the Indian sub-continent were excluded. By contrast many of the current members of the ACP group, including most of the Commonwealth Caribbean, fall within the definition of middle-income developing countries. It is therefore likely that EDF funds will continue to be increasingly concentrated upon the African members of the group.

Similarly the demands of the WTO have had consequences beyond those affecting the banana industry. The need for WTO compatibility underlies the move towards reciprocal regional free trade agreements - Economic Partnership Agreements (EPA) - under the new Cotonou Convention. Only the low-income ACP states will be able to benefit from a continuation of the non-reciprocal trade preferences that they currently enjoy. However even the value of these concessions will probably be eroded by the likely general reduction of tariffs under the new Millennium Round of trade negotiations. For the States of the Commonwealth Caribbean reciprocal EPAs are likely to prove the only option. Faced with a conflict between its historic commitments to the ACP states and its new obligations to the WTO, it is the latter that have come to dominate, especially as they involve the far more significant economic interests of the EU's relationship with the United States. Thus while the development commitments of the EU will continue to be met through sustained trade preferences and aid funding for the low-income states, both ACP and non-ACP, the middle-income ACP states, which includes most of the Commonwealth Caribbean, are likely to find themselves increasingly marginalised.

With the demise of the Rum Protocol and the phasing out of the Banana Protocol, only the Sugar Protocol might appear to have any long term future. Although the Sugar Protocol is unique, in that it has a separate legal persona and is not tied to the Lomé Conventions, its infinite duration is qualified by the ability of any party to terminate the agreement at two years notice (Art. 10). The EU has already indicated its intention to renegotiate the agreement in the context of the establishment of the EPAs under Cotonou. This may be inevitable as the new free-trade agreements must cover 'substantially all trade' to meet the requirements of the WTO (Art. 24). Such an agreement would open up the domestic sugar markets of the Commonwealth Caribbean to competition from subsidised Community sugar beet producers. But ironically a further threat to the Protocol arises from the need to reduce these same sugar beet subsidies. As the guaranteed prices offered under the Protocol are linked to those offered to Community suppliers, the increasing pressure to reform the CAP, especially with the prospective enlargement of the Community, is likely to erode their value. Already with world sugar prices depressed the EU is hitting the subsidy limit for its own sugar exports, which it undertook to observe under the Uruguay Round, and hence there is pressure on the volume of imports and the CAP support price.

The future of the Sugar Protocol and the transitional arrangements for bananas and rum, will be the product of the same interaction of economic and political interests as in the past. Within the EU the demands of current and future 'domestic' producers of sugar beet, bananas and rum, will be in conflict with the interests of the ACP producers and the EU traders and processors who support their imports. Member States will also, to varying degrees, be addressing the interests of their domestic consumers and the budgetary implications of the trade policy that is adopted, especially as it interacts with the CAP. Externally the broader trade interests of the Community will interact with those of its other major trading partners, such as the USA, within the context of the WTO. The trade preferences of the ACP group are also likely to be eroded by the general movement towards trade liberalisation under the Millennium Round, by the establishment of free-trade agreements (e.g. with Mercosur: South America), individual Association Agreements and from the review of the General System of Preferences offered by the EU to developing countries in 2004.

As we have seen the Commodity Protocols have been of considerable value to a number of Commonwealth Caribbean economies, indeed it could be argued that as a group they have been one of the major beneficiaries. For those economies where a particular commodity dominated their economies, the industry not only provided employment and export earnings but it also made a major contribution to the economic and social infrastructure. For the banana producers the regular transport links provided by the reefer ships has been crucial for some islands. High transport costs remain a major economic disadvantage for many of these economies. In Guyana the sugar industry has been responsible for the provision of some social services including housing and health services. However critics have argued that the Protocols have also created a dependence upon commodity exports where these States have little prospect of being internationally competitive and have inhibited diversification. However for this argument to be sustained it is necessary to address the economic problems that are peculiar to the smaller island economies and the isolated continental States of Guyana and Belize.

These countries small domestic markets limits the potential for economies of scale in production and therefore domestic manufacturing.

Their geographical isolation raises transport costs and their small population limits the skills available. Public administration suffers from similar problems of high relative costs and a shortage of specialist skills. The result has been economies characterised by balance of payments deficits, public sector deficits, unstable growth, high unemployment and a dependence upon remittances from overseas workers. Whatever the weaknesses in terms of international competitiveness of some of the commodities produced in these islands, these industries still offer a comparative advantage relative to many alternative activities.

Nonetheless the need for diversification has been recognised for some time and governments have turned in particular to tourism and offshore finance. Unfortunately tourism is becoming an increasingly competitive industry in the Caribbean, is vulnerable to world recessions and may make only a limited contribution to the domestic economy. A reliance upon foreign capital for development and the need for food imports limits the benefits to the balance of payments, while the environmental impact can be significant, e.g. in provision of adequate water supplies. The increasing importance of the cruise industry, rather than long-stay visitors, also limits the financial benefit. Meanwhile the governments of those States hosting offshore finance centres are coming under increasing pressure from the OECD to bring their regulations and corporate tax regime into line with those of the rest of the international community, raising the prospect that it will undermine their relative attractiveness to international capital.

But other opportunities for diversification are emerging. Developments in information technology, for example, are eroding the economic disadvantages of isolated States and offering the potential for data processing or software development. Central to any strategy for diversification must be the role of the private sector and it is clear from the Cotonou Agreement that creating the conditions that will foster a dynamic private sector is fundamental to the EU's development policy. The attraction of foreign capital and technology and the encouragement of small and medium sized export-orientated enterprises is seen as crucial to the achievement of sustainable long run growth.

The particular environmental problems of small island developing States (SIDS) were addressed at a 1994 UN conference in Barbados which resulted in a Programme of Action (POA). Not only do they face the short-run disruption of events such as hurricanes, but they are also presented with the pressures upon fisheries, coral reefs and fresh water resources from population growth and tourism developments and the long term threat of rising sea levels with global warming. The Barbados POA identified fourteen priority areas including climate change, natural and environmental disasters, freshwater resources, waste management, coastal and marine resources, biodiversity and tourism. As a signatory of the Barbados Programme the EU will need to take account of these issues in its future relations with the Caribbean. NIPs and regional aid programmes will need to take account of these requirements. Capacity building in local administrations to properly monitor projects and environmental evaluation of tourism projects, are just two areas that should reflect these priorities. The EU's support for regional integration in the Caribbean can also make an important contribution. Issues such as fisheries and marine pollution can only be tackled at a regional level.

Although defined as middle-income developing countries, the limited available evidence suggests a relatively high incidence of poverty. This leaves a significant part of the population especially vulnerable to the environmental and economic shocks to which these islands are particularly exposed. Well developed poverty reduction programmes, with an emphasise upon education and housing, should remain a priority in EU assistance. But to deliver these programmes public administration requires strengthening. Enhanced regional cooperation may be important in contributing to the increased effectiveness in the delivery of some public services. This sense of a common regional identity is likely to have been enhanced by the Commonwealth Caribbean's coordinated attempts to defend the Commodity Protocols and are likely to be further reinforced by the need to negotiate a regional EPA under Cotonou. Finally, although most of the States have maintained reasonably sound public finances, they are dependent upon foreign aid and concessional and commercial borrowing for the funding of public sector investment and disaster recovery. Good debt management will be essential if unsustainable external debt burdens are to be avoided.

This book has reviewed the post-colonial Commodity Protocols of the European Union and has charted their demise. There are serious doubts as to the future of the Cotonou/Lomé Conventions themselves and the continued special treatment of the ACP group by the European Community. Given the ACP group's arbitrary historical antecedents and the desire of the EU to emphasise regional agreements, there may also be a question mark hanging over the coherence of the group itself. Although the unity of the ACP States gives them greater weight in negotiations with the EU, the interests of the individual States are not necessarily shared. The Caribbean has been particularly active and successful in enhancing its influence through the ACP group, but the limitations of this strategy have become clear in the banana negotiations. Meanwhile the EU itself may, in the foreseeable future, come to regard the Caribbean as merely an adjunct to its Latin American policy, shifting its attention away from the Caribbean grouping of the ACP and towards the wider 25 member Association of Caribbean States, which also includes Mexico, Colombia, Venezuela and the States of Central America. Perhaps the most important lesson to be learnt from this history of the Commodity Protocols is that the Caribbean States must now look to the strengthening of their own regional organisations if they are to defend their interests in the new world trading order.

Index